The Open University

Block 2
The European Reformation

Ole Peter Grell, Rosemary O'Day, Anne Laurence and
Donna Loftus

This publication forms part of the Open University module A200 *Exploring History: Medieval to Modern 1400–1900*. Details of this and other Open University modules can be obtained from the Student Registration and Enquiry Service, The Open University, PO Box 197, Milton Keynes MK7 6BJ, United Kingdom (tel. +44 (0)845 300 60 90; email general-enquiries@open.ac.uk).

Alternatively, you may visit the Open University website at www.open.ac.uk where you can learn more about the wide range of modules and packs offered at all levels by The Open University.

To purchase a selection of Open University materials visit www.ouw.co.uk, or contact Open University Worldwide, Walton Hall, Milton Keynes MK7 6AA, United Kingdom for a brochure (tel. +44 (0)1908 858793; fax +44 (0)1908 858787; email ouw-customer-services@open.ac.uk).

The Open University
Walton Hall
Milton Keynes
MK7 6AA

First published 2007

Second edition 2011

Edited and designed by The Open University.

Printed and bound in the United Kingdom by Bell & Bain Ltd, Glasgow

ISBN 978 1 8487 3909 3

2.1

CONTENTS

WHAT YOU NEED TO STUDY THIS BLOCK

- Units 5–8
- *Module Companion*
- *Media Guide*
- *Visual Sources Book*
- Set book: Wallace, P.G. (2004) *The Long European Reformation: Religion, Political Conflict and the Search for Conformity, 1350–1750*, London, Palgrave Macmillan
- Anthology: Gibbons, R.C. (ed.) (2007) *Exploring History 1400–1900: An Anthology of Primary Sources*, Manchester, Manchester University Press/ Milton Keynes, The Open University
- A200 website
- TMA 02

Learning outcomes

When you have finished this block, you should be able to:

- understand the nature and importance of the Reformation, particularly within the context of two of our themes, state formation, and beliefs and ideologies

- use a textbook to help you to understand events and processes during the Reformation, and to interpret primary sources

- appreciate and discuss the importance of aspects of the historiography of the Reformation and of the methods and approaches employed by historians to interpret what happened and why

- 'read' a variety of primary texts, both written and visual, with confidence, to contribute to your understanding of the themes.

Anne Laurence and Donna Loftus

INTRODUCTION

The subject of this block is the sixteenth-century Protestant Reformation. In such a secular age as ours, you might ask why we should take any interest in a split within Christianity that took place around 500 years ago. The answer is that it is regarded as a crucial movement in European history, a period after which everything was different. In that sense, we might even call it a revolution, if by this we mean far-reaching change in the social order. In this week's work you will come to understand why the Reformation is associated with such transformation. You will not be surprised to learn that a process central to European history such as the Reformation is much debated by historians. As you saw in Block 1, historians often debate the causes and consequences of historical events, and interpretations can vary according to the types of issues they address and the kinds of sources they use. You will be introduced to the skills that will help you to make good use of the set book for this module, Peter Wallace, *The Long European Reformation*. In this block, as well as learning about the Reformation, you will be asked to think further about historical debate and disagreement and how different approaches to the past produce different kinds of history writing. There is, as you will see, plenty of scope for discussion.

WHY STUDY THE REFORMATION?

What was the Reformation? It was a process that took place in the sixteenth century but that had important resonances in later periods. The essence of the process was the challenge mounted to the hegemony of the Catholic Church over western and southern Europe by Christians who believed that the authority exercised by the church over belief, education and intellectual debate, and by the papacy over European rulers, was not justified by the word of God as understood from the Bible. It was also a challenge to the Catholic Church's role in community life. Ultimately that challenge resulted not only in the formation of several Protestant churches, but also in the transformation of the Catholic Church. As such, some historians prefer to represent that turbulent period by using the plural, 'Reformations'. In this module we will use the singular, but you will be asked to consider the diverse impact of the Reformation on European religion, society and politics.

The Reformation was both a religious revolution and a profound cultural and intellectual shift. Late medieval Europe shared the universal Christianity of the Catholic Church (as you know from Block 1, 'catholic' means 'universal'). The reformers of the sixteenth century issued a radical challenge to the authority of the Catholic Church, its traditions and beliefs, and to the papacy.

The reformers wanted to replace them with a Christianity that drew its authority solely from the Bible, from the word of God, rather than from earthly customs. This had implications beyond religion and its practice: it deeply affected the ways in which people thought about the economy, and understood relationships between individuals and the societies in which they lived. For example, as you will see in the discussion of the Peasants' War of 1524–25, the intellectual and theological debates on authority were bound up with questions about people's social and economic relationships. Since theology was the primary medium for intellectual exchange in medieval Europe, the Reformation also offered a challenge to older ways of comprehending the material and abstract worlds.

Reflecting on these questions has profoundly influenced later historians and political scientists interested in looking at the long-term development of European history. Some scholars have associated the Reformation with the emergence of beliefs and practices that are linked to modernity, such as individualism and capitalism. For example, many of them judge that the Reformation was critical in shifting the balance of prosperity and economic development from southern Europe (the Mediterranean world) to northern Europe (the Atlantic world). Most famously, Max Weber, writing in 1905, attributed the growth of capitalism in northern Europe to the 'Protestant ethic' that developed after the Reformation. In his famous essay 'The Protestant ethic and the spirit of capitalism' (1904–05), Weber argued that Calvinism encouraged the move towards modernity and the growth of capitalism. This was due to the particular economic ethics of Calvinism, which Weber saw as an unintended consequence of the doctrine of predestination. In Weber's view, predestination resulted in an anxiety about salvation. This in turn brought about a strong work ethic, with an emphasis on wealth creation as 'proof' of being among the chosen.

Weber's thesis was translated into English and published in a book in 1930 and has since provoked considerable debate. His arguments have been challenged by historians who, as Wallace notes, have questioned the place of the Reformation in history and the extent to which it can be seen as a modernising force. Instead, more recent histories have shown that the Reformation needs to be understood on its own terms and its diverse effects explored through studies that examine the links between religion, culture, society and politics (Wallace, pp. 5–6).

You can see that the subject of the sixteenth-century Reformation provides historians with plenty of material with which to debate the origins and significance of the process, to discuss what actually constituted reform and to locate the origins of such significant ideas as capitalism, individualism and modern science. In this block we shall look at the ways in which historians have engaged in debate through different kinds of historical writing.

Beliefs in history

In Unit 1 of Block 1 you were encouraged to put yourself, as much as possible, into the mindset of the people you are studying. This applies too, when you are studying the history of the Reformation. Many of the beliefs people held in the past, religious or not, may appear to you to be strange. But it is important to remember that they may not have seemed so at the time. On the other hand, if you share some of the beliefs that you encounter, you need to stand back and consider them in the context of the period you are studying. Then, as now, people understood the world in their own terms. Human beings seek meaning in the events and developments taking place around them, especially those over which they have little or no control. In earlier times, supernatural intervention might have been the only way of providing an explanation for such occurrences as meteorological catastrophes, disease and unexpected death. A major upheaval in the church, in people's established beliefs and practices, had profound effects on many aspects of society – so profound that people were prepared to kill one another in defence of their beliefs.

HOW DO HISTORIANS STUDY THE REFORMATION?

In Block 1 you explored a number of primary sources and saw how historians can use these sources to help them understand the period in which they were created. Written documents and artefacts from the period can do much more than simply supply information. They can also be used to tell us how contemporaries understood events and processes. In Block 1, Unit 3, you also explored historical debate and historiography. This block takes these aspects of study further by looking in greater detail at the ways in which historians write about the past and how their approach to a topic influences the kind of history they produce. This is to encourage you to develop critical faculties when studying historians' work – work that we call secondary because it was written subsequent to the subject of study.

Primary and secondary sources

Before we consider historical method it is first necessary to think about the nature of historical sources. Think for a moment about what you would do if you wanted to find out something about the Reformation. You might look it up on the internet or in an encyclopedia. But if you wanted a deeper understanding, you would probably turn to one or more books on the subject. From where do the authors of these books get their knowledge? The answer may well be from other books. But the author of a detailed, specialised book on the Reformation, or some aspect of it, will have drawn on materials belonging to the time of the Reformation itself – theologians' declarations and polemical pamphlets (we are in the age of printing), correspondence, diaries, royal decrees and laws. Such things are the basic 'raw material' of history: primary sources – sources that came into existence within the actual period being studied.

The books written later, by historians drawing on primary sources, are termed secondary sources. As you know from the *Module Companion*, in the study of history, the distinction between secondary sources (books, articles, factual television programmes presented by historians) and primary sources (materials originating within the period being studied) is absolutely crucial. Making this distinction is not, however, always as straightforward as it may seem.

The next exercise gives you the opportunity to try to distinguish between primary and secondary sources, but first let us clarify a few points:

1   A source in the form of a printed book is not necessarily a secondary source. A printed book, pamphlet or newspaper, if it was originally produced within the period being studied, is a primary source. Look at the date on which it was *first* written or published. Many books in the sixteenth and seventeenth centuries were published long after they were written, nevertheless they are still primary sources if they were produced within the period being studied.

2   Documentary primary sources in their original form are most usually found in specialist libraries and archives, such as the British Library in London, the Bibliothèque Nationale in Paris, or record offices such as those run by counties, provinces and dioceses. Printed and online primary sources make manuscript materials more widely available. There are also anthologies of primary sources, collections of specially edited (and, where necessary, translated) documents, such as your Anthology.

3   Although historical research requires consideration of primary sources, researchers have to use secondary sources as well. Secondary sources give historians knowledge of what other experts in the field have concluded. They also provide pointers to sources to study and the archives where these sources may be found, as well as to possible issues and problems. They save historians from duplicating work and help them frame the questions that guide their research. Historians, for all their disagreements, work collaboratively and build on each other's research.

EXERCISE

Look at Sources 1–4 below. For each, an author, a date of publication, a title and a publisher is given. Below each source is a brief synopsis, such as you might find on the back of a book or in a book catalogue. As you will see, all the sources are concerned with the Reformation, or aspects of it. Using the information you are given about each source, can you work out which are primary and which are secondary?

1   Anonymous (1680) *A true account of the rise and growth of the Reformation, or the progress of the Protestant religion. Setting forth the lives and dying speeches of the first and most famous doctors of the Protestant church, their constancy and stedfastness in the same to their deaths and cruel martyrdomes they suffered by those bloody cruel papists, and now printed and published as a thankful remembrance of God's goodness to all protestants in these three kingdomes of England, Scotland and Ireland, and necessary to be set up in every house and*

family. And recommended to all persons by these reverend divines, Mr. W.I. Mr. R. B. Mr. N.V. [London], That the reader be not deceived by a counterfeit sheet (full of many falshoods) in imitation of this, the true sheet is only printed and sold by Ioshua Conyers at the Black Raven in Duck Lane.

This broadside, single sheet, was almost certainly published as part of a propaganda campaign mounted in England in 1680, at the end of Charles II's reign, as a result of anxiety about the growing influence of Catholics in the government.

2   Leopold von Ranke (1845–47) *History of the Reformation in Germany*, 3 vols (trans. Sarah Austin), London, Longman Green.

Leopold von Ranke (1795–1886) first published this book in German with the title *Deutsche Geschichte im Zeitalter der Reformation*; it appeared in six volumes published between 1839 and 1847. Ranke is regarded as the father of modern academic history, pioneering the use of historical documents: he used archives in Germany to study the Reformation through official documents and correspondence between officials and local people. He believed that the truth could be revealed by a close study of primary sources. Sarah Austin née Taylor (1793–1867) translated a substantial proportion of the original six volumes. In the introduction to one of her translations, she said that she was presenting both the English and the original German of the footnotes to show 'how the author has lived with his heroes, and listened to their homely and expressive language' (Ranke, 1845, p. iv).

3   Rosemary O'Day (1986) *The Debate on the English Reformation*, London, Methuen.

Rosemary O'Day (1945–) is emeritus professor of history at The Open University (she retired in 2010). This book is one of a series on debates in different areas of history and is primarily a discussion of the historiography of the Reformation in England – that is to say, a history of how the history of the Reformation has been written. In the early chapters, O'Day explains how, between the sixteenth and the nineteenth centuries, people used the history of the Reformation to support various causes – such as giving political rights to Roman Catholics. In the later chapters, O'Day has synthesised the more detailed work of other historians that may be inaccessible to students because it appears in scholarly journals or is written in another language. This work refers to the original writings of reformers.

4   Diarmaid MacCulloch (2003) *Reformation: Europe's House Divided 1490–1700*, London, Allen Lane.

Diarmaid MacCulloch (1951–) is professor of the history of the church in the Oxford University theology faculty and a greatly respected historian of the Reformation. His biography of Thomas Cranmer, who was the archbishop of Canterbury during the most turbulent period of the Reformation in England and was executed in 1556, won many prizes (MacCulloch, 1996). He also wrote *A History of Christianity: The First Three Thousand Years* (MacCulloch, 2009), to accompany a successful BBC TV series. In his preface to *Reformation: Europe's House Divided 1490–1700*, MacCulloch claimed that his own personal experience of religion made him well placed to both understand and critique those he was studying. He comes from a Scottish Episcopalian and Anglican family, though he states 'I do not now personally subscribe to any form of religious dogma (although I do remember with some affection what it was like to do so)'.

Spend about 15 minutes on this exercise.

SPECIMEN ANSWER

1   Although this is not a primary source for the sixteenth-century religious Reformation, it is a primary source if you are studying the consequences of the Reformation in England in the late seventeenth century. It is also a primary source if you think the Reformation was a series of debates about religion that continued into the seventeenth century. In both these cases, the source was written within the period being studied.

2   This is a secondary source: a piece of history writing composed from the primary sources that Ranke studied in German archives. It is a primary source if you are interested in historiography and the history of written history.

3   This is a secondary source. However, O'Day has treated histories of the Reformation as primary sources because her study is of the historiography of the Reformation.

4   This is a secondary source.

DISCUSSION

Primary sources are produced in the period that is being studied. However, the definition of a primary source is complicated by the historian's aim or purpose. In the examples given above, the definition of a source can change according to the purpose of the historian. For example, Ranke is a primary source for historians of nineteenth-century history writing – as you will learn in Block 5 – and a rather outdated secondary source for historians of the Reformation. The anonymous tract from 1680 shows how the recent past can be presented as history and used to serve a political purpose in the present.

EXERCISE

Look again at the authors' details, the titles, publication details and synopses of the books listed above. Read the synopses carefully and consider how these writers have approached the subject. What position is each author writing from? How can we evaluate their reliability?

Spend about 10 minutes on this exercise.

SPECIMEN ANSWER

1   The broadside is anonymous and, despite its claims to be true, it is clearly propaganda. It charts the history of Protestant martyrs to promote anti-Catholic sentiment. It would not offer a reliable account of the Reformation; however, historians could use it to study the way in which early histories of the Reformation were used in politico-religious campaigns.

2   Ranke claims that from studying primary sources the historian can produce a true account. This suggests that his book provides genuine insight into the thoughts and feelings of those who lived through the Reformation in Germany. But how real are Ranke's claims? To write his book he would have had to select sources, describe them and put them into a narrative. His book was originally written in German and translated into English. Does this process produce a true account of the past?

3   O'Day's account is not close to events and nor does it claim to be. It offers a critical account of published histories based on a detailed knowledge of the

contemporary scholarship on the Reformation and the circumstances in which each work was written. As such it is a reliable account of the historiography, using works on the Reformation as its primary sources.

4   MacCulloch's history is also based on a detailed knowledge of the Reformation as a result of expertise based on scholarship. However, his claims to authority are based on his personal as well as his professional experience. He claims that his experience of religious belief and later agnosticism has helped him to interpret primary sources with empathy – they enable him to understand the beliefs of the people he is researching.

DISCUSSION

The answer to this question of the reliability of sources is not as simple as it might at first appear. Claims to truth and reliability can be made according to the author's closeness to events – think for example about the power of an eyewitness account. Claims to truth can also be made through the author's distance from events – the ability to stand back, weigh up arguments and assess the significance of events with objectivity. However, as the exercise also shows, historians can use their knowledge of a subject to assess the reliability of all sources – primary and secondary. Information such as the author, the date, the nature of the evidence used, and an awareness of how the writer puts this together can help you to evaluate the usefulness of a source.

The books by O'Day and MacCulloch are scholarly: the authors' statements are referenced in footnotes or endnotes, providing details of the sources used, whether primary or secondary, and both authors have used a substantial number of sources. It is a feature of the history of the sixteenth and seventeenth centuries that historical research is undertaken by both historians and theologians; it is also a measure of how difficult it is to separate the study of the church in society in this period from the study of its beliefs.

READING WALLACE

Having looked at some of the different kinds of book we might find on the Reformation, turn now to your set book, Wallace, *The Long European Reformation*.

Before starting to read a book or article, there are a number of questions that you need to ask about it:

1   What do we know about the author?
2   When was the book or article published?
3   What does the author say about his or her intention for the book or article?
4   What kinds of sources does the author make use of?
5   Is there anything else that might tell us what kind of a book or article it is?

EXERCISE

Try to answer these questions for Wallace. Look at the cover, the publication details, the notes for the introduction and the select bibliography, then read pp. 1–8.

Spend about 30 minutes on this exercise.

1   We learn from the cover that Peter G. Wallace works at an American university and that his previous work has been on seventeenth-century Colmar. (Colmar was part of the Holy Roman Empire but subsequently became part of France.)

2   The book was first published in 2004.

3   Wallace tells us (p. 3) that this book is the account of the Reformation he has arrived at in trying to reconcile his own preconceptions with the accounts of earlier historians.

4   Wallace uses a wide selection of secondary sources (monographs – that is, detailed, scholarly books by a single author; collections of essays by multiple authors; a few articles in scholarly journals; surveys). But he draws not only on works of religious history or studies of a particular period or country, but also on works that address broader historical problems, such as *Social Memory* (Fentress and Wickham, 1992), *In Defence of History* (Evans, 2000 [1997]) and *Imagined Communities* (Anderson, 2006 [1991]). He does not make extensive use of primary sources, but many of the secondary sources he uses will have been based on extensive archival research.

5   The book is in a British series called 'European History in Perspective'. Other titles in the same series are listed on the reverse of the first title page. You can see that they are all on the 'big subjects' of European history.

Putting information together as you did in the exercise above helps you to evaluate a source and fit it in to the wider historiography. Wallace clearly states his position, his influences and the kinds of traditional approaches to the history of Reformation that he wishes to challenge.

All books about history are artefacts – that is, they are things that have been produced by a human being. This person has his or her own beliefs and preconceptions, as well as knowledge of different kinds of historical source and of the literature on the subject on which they are writing.

So, as well as learning to extract points of information, it is important to learn to read critically. 'Reading critically' does not mean offering adverse criticism on interpretations or style; rather, it means reading with discrimination, understanding how what you are reading fits into the range of different kinds of history writing. Understanding how historians approach the subjects of their study is integral to the study of history.

THEMES

You know that the themes of the module are state formation, beliefs and ideologies, and producers and consumers, and that these three designations also roughly correspond to different subdisciplines of history (political; cultural, religious and intellectual; social and economic). This block is dominated by the theme of beliefs and ideologies, but both state formation and producers and consumers played a significant role in the changes that took place as a result of the Reformation.

In this section, you will be using the set book by Wallace to explore how the module themes relate to this block. To do this you will need to look back at the extracts from Wallace on which you made notes in Block 1 (pp. 25–53 and 54–63) and complete your reading of Chapter 2. You may also wish to remind yourself of the early history of Christianity, which is covered in the Introduction to Wallace (pp. 8–21; you skim read this in Block 1, Unit 4).

Because studying history means doing a lot of reading, you need to develop, if you do not already have them, skills in reading in different ways, at different paces and for different purposes. This will also help you in your note-taking. If you read everything very slowly, taking notes on everything that catches your eye, it will not only take you a long time, but also make it harder for you to single out what is important.

But how do you judge what is important? The answer depends on the purpose for which you are reading. Are you reading to get a general sense of the subject or to answer a specific question (for example, for a TMA)? If the latter, you would read and take notes on the points that are relevant to your TMA as you go along. In the next exercise you are asked to relate historical developments to the module themes. You have already made notes on some sections of Wallace that relate to the question, so you will need to either look back at your notes or re-read key passages to identify the points you think are relevant. The exercise also requires you to complete your reading of Chapter 2. You are not asked to provide a lot of detail in your answer to this exercise, so you do not need to take detailed notes.

EXERCISE

First, look back at the notes you took on Wallace, pp. 25–53 and 54–63, then finish reading Chapter 2 (pp. 64–81) and answer the following question:

Of the various historical developments identified by Wallace, which correspond to each of the three themes of the module?

One or two examples for each theme will suffice.

Spend about 1 hour on this exercise.

SPECIMEN ANSWER

Producers and consumers

Wallace starts Chapter 1 with a discussion of the Black Death and its impact on the agricultural economy – the diminution in the population of producers and consumers and the changes to the way in which producers worked. You will remember this from Block 1. Note (p. 25) that religious officials called for special church services to avert catastrophe.

State formation

On p. 30 Wallace discusses the instability of many European states as a result of dynastic struggles and conflict. He also notes how the functions of the state were shaped by the private interest of the ruling class. The governing elite were drawn from the same networks and this allowed for interconnections between state and church. The significance of senior churchmen in royal service ensured that that state and religion shared Christian ideologies of rule. The concept of Christendom brought together church and state (pp. 18, 31). Religious and secular power were fused in different ways at different periods (pp. 15, 39) and the spread of the organised church brought its influence to bear on all aspects of life (p. 34). Reform movements seem sometimes to have been associated with an embryonic form of nationalism, as in the kingdoms of Bohemia and France (pp. 60, 72). By the late fifteenth century, the hegemony of the papacy seems to have been giving way to greater power for secular rulers (pp. 71–74).

Beliefs and ideologies

At the beginning of Chapter 2, Wallace discusses the emergence of a doctrinal orthodoxy which defined what was not orthodox as heretical. This is really the first time that he discusses religious belief in any detail (though in Chapter 1 he discussed political ideologies such as papal monarchy and conciliarism). But he also construes heresy as a 'manifestation of political and ideological dissent' (p. 56). In pp. 54–60, he discusses spiritual renewal, but in the rest of the chapter he ties this in with the emergence of different kinds of reform movement, not all of which were heretical.

DISCUSSION

Did you notice that politics, religion, society and the economy are intimately bound up with one another, to the point where it is often difficult to disentangle them?

As Wallace makes clear, Christianity, from its inception, challenged both the Roman secular government and the Jewish religion. The common feature was the challenge posed by the new religion to both political and religious authority. By the time it reached Europe, Christianity was devising its own sources of authority, in the New Testament and through its own institutions. The government of Christians by the Holy Roman Emperor and the papacy combined temporal and spiritual rule. The Catholic Church was a kind of quasi-state, with the pope as both a spiritual ruler and a temporal ruler of the Vatican. The church had extensive lands, large numbers of tenants and was able to raise taxes (see for example pp. 18, 33, 41, 43, 48, 76).

There are some places where some historians might challenge Wallace's views. On p. 26 he says: 'By 1300, from nearly any steeple top in Western Europe, an observer could see church towers in all directions'. This was certainly not the case in much of Scotland and Ireland, in central France, central Spain, Scandinavia and north-eastern Germany (Treasure, 1985, p. 7).

In the first two chapters you have read, Wallace pays little attention to the nature of spirituality or matters of personal faith. His book is a work of history, examining the role of faith and its adherents in the long-term political and economic history of western Europe, rather than a study of the personal beliefs of individuals. It is hard to know what the beliefs of individuals were in an age when few people could record their thoughts and when the survival rate of documents to the present is at any rate low: the great majority of evidence we have for their beliefs is in their acts and material culture. The passage on p. 33 should remind you of the film on parish churches on DVD 1 showing how church furnishings reflect changes in religious practices which arose from different doctrinal interpretations.

It is easy to be overwhelmed by the detail of the book – the long lists of popes, the disputes with secular rulers, the organisational changes in the church. Within this detail, however, lie nuggets of historical judgement, what historians call Wallace's 'argument'. One important example of this is his statement on p. 52 that 'the Reformation was not inevitable'; another is his perception that recent historical work has tended to the view that fifteenth-century Christianity was not in decay and waiting for reform (p. 63). Here Wallace reminds you not to be tempted to put the Reformation into broader narratives of progress that see it as a part of the modernising of religion, the state and society in the years before the Enlightenment.

Finally, this block is about the Reformation of the sixteenth century, but it will be apparent to you that there have been earlier reform movements in Roman Catholicism. Some of these were plainly tied up with the politics of the period, but others argued that the reformers were returning to the original 'pure' roots of Christianity (see for example, pp. 19, 21, 37, 44, 47, 52, 54–60). Wallace's argument fits with the thrust of Block 1: you need to understand the Reformation as part of the history of Europe 'from medieval to modern': to do so, however, means understanding it in its own terms.

CONCLUSION

Historians and their sources

Historians not only produce different kinds of writing but also use sources in different ways. They might disagree over the interpretation of documents; the significance of an event or series of events; or the relative impact of different developments in precipitating changes. Different accounts of the past can be produced as a result of different perspectives. Historians who wish to write about the Reformation in relation to government and politics will produce a different sort of history from those who wish to explore the reactions of normal people in everyday life. You will see examples of these different approaches to the history of the Reformation later in the block and, in the section on whether the Reformation in sixteenth-century England was a popular Reformation, you will see how different approaches can produce different interpretations of the Reformation.

What is important to remember is that most historians are not simply trying to describe the passage of past events. They are concerned with *analysing* evidence and using it to consider continuities in the past as well as *evaluating* the extent of change. To do this they need to have a thorough understanding of how their evidence came into being. (If you are in doubt about the meaning of terms such as 'evaluate' and 'analyse', these are explained in the *TMA Booklet*.)

Understanding the nature of secondary sources and the processes involved in evaluating them will help you to assess their value to your study. When we dub sources 'secondary' we do not mean that they are unimportant – far from it. By studying primary sources closely and setting them in the context of current debates, modern historians help us to understand the past better than we would if we were to rely solely on close reading of individual primary sources.

The Reformation and its lasting importance

At the beginning of this unit, we observed that historians concentrate on the Reformation because it was a crucial movement in European history that generated great change. As you continue your study of this block, you will see why the Reformation was so important at the time it took place; in Block 3 you will look at the resonances 100 years later. The issues you encounter in your study of the Reformation will re-emerge at various points throughout the module. Christianity also had a significant part to play both in justifying slavery and in the abolitionist movement, the subject of Block 4. The division that emerged as a result of the Reformation created Catholic and Protestant Europe (broadly Spain, Italy, Portugal, France, Belgium, Poland and Ireland on the one hand and Germany, the Netherlands, Scandinavia, Switzerland and Britain on the other), which coloured deeply the nationalist movements that emerged in many of those countries in the nineteenth century, the subject of Block 5. A number of these states acquired overseas possessions outside Europe, which were often associated with Christian missionary activity. Catholic Spain had Catholic colonies in South and Central America; French colonies in Africa and elsewhere were served by Catholic missionaries; British and Dutch colonies all over the world were served by Protestant missions. Some of the impact of this is to be seen in Block 6.

REFERENCES

Anderson, B. (2006 [1991]) *Imagined Communities: Reflections on the Origin and Spread of Nationalism*, revised edn, London, Verso.

Evans, R.J. (2000 [1997]) *In Defence of History*, London, Granta.

Fentress, J. and Wickham, C. (1992) *Social Memory*, Oxford, Blackwell.

MacCulloch, D. (1996) *Thomas Cranmer: A Life*, New Haven, Yale University Press.

MacCulloch, D. (2009) *A History of Christianity: The First Three Thousand Years*, London, Allen Lane top

Ranke, L. von (1845) *History of the Reformation in Germany*, 2nd edn (trans. S. Austin), London, Longman Green.

Treasure, G. (1985) *The Making of Modern Europe 1648–1780*, London, Methuen.

Weber, M. (1930) *The Protestant Ethic and the Spirit of Capitalism* (trans. T. Parsons), London, Allen and Unwin.

Ole Peter Grell

INTRODUCTION

The Protestant Reformation in Europe was a process that broke up western Christianity, which until then had provided the religious and ideological foundation for the whole of western society since the early Middle Ages. If you had not heard about such major figures of the Protestant Reformation as Martin Luther and John Calvin before studying A200, you will at least have had some knowledge of the English Reformation, especially of Henry VIII's break with Rome and the Catholic Church.

This unit will introduce you to the major challenges that Luther and the early reformers presented to early modern church and society. It will give you some insight into how and why the Reformation succeeded with such speed in north-western Europe. It will do this through the set book by Wallace and a selection of primary sources from the Anthology, which together will give you an understanding of what the Reformation was about and why it proved so appealing. Much of what you have already read in Unit 4 will assist you here. You have been introduced to the main Catholic beliefs and should have a clear understanding of the Catholic Church's claim to hold a monopoly on access to salvation, through the sacraments of the church, and that individuals could improve their chances of salvation through acts of piety, such as pilgrimages, acts of charity and the purchase of masses. You will also have learnt that the period leading up to the Reformation had already seen the emergence of a number of movements for reform, such as the Waldensians, the Lollards and the Hussites. Likewise, you will have understood that papal control over the Catholic Church had been challenged during the fifteenth century: from within by those who wanted the church to be controlled and led by general councils rather than the pope, and from without by lay rulers and princes. This resulted, as you have seen, in the Great Schism and in some cases forced popes to concede control over national churches to ruling monarchs. (Figure 6.1 shows how Protestantism had spread in central Europe by about 1570.)

You might therefore conclude that the Catholic Church was a much weakened institution by the time Martin Luther first challenged it in 1517, but that, as we shall see, was not necessarily the case.

In this unit you will look in more detail at the challenges that Luther and other early reformers posed to the church, at why the Reformation took hold so fast in northern Europe and at why it appealed to such large numbers of people. You will also look at some different kinds of historical writing by comparing Wallace's perspective on the Reformation with that presented in the unit.

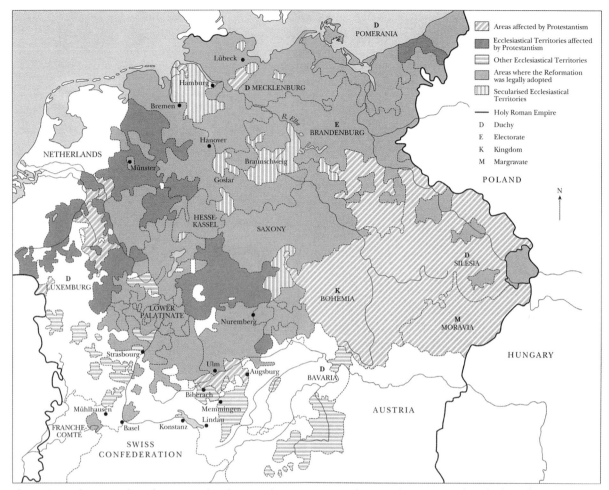

Figure 6.1 The expansion of Protestantism in central Europe, *c.*1570, from Mark Greengrass (1998) *The European Reformation, c.1500–1618*, London & New York: Longman, pp. 376–7, map 8

As you have seen from your reading of sections of the set book by Wallace, western Christianity was undergoing a process of reform before the Reformation, instigated from several different directions: secular rulers, monastic orders, theologians and church officers concerned with church government. So what made the Reformation of the sixteenth century different from these earlier movements? Humanism and printing can be identified as two of the most significant features of the sixteenth century that were absent from earlier reform movements, but there were others.

EXERCISE

Now look at the notes you took from your reading of pp. 54–67 in the set book by Wallace in Unit 5. What do you think were the major areas of renewal within the Catholic Church in the century leading up to the evangelical challenge launched by Luther?

Spend about 20 minutes on this exercise.

Major areas of renewal include: the emergence of many reform-minded preachers who openly criticised the church; the reforms of many monastic orders, bringing them back to their founding principles of poverty and spirituality; and a renewed emphasis on orthodox lay piety. Furthermore, local cults underwent a revival while the number of pious endowments increased considerably.

Among the reform-minded preachers referred to by Wallace is Geiler von Kaysersberg, who became one of the outstanding preachers of reform in the Holy Roman Empire on the eve of the Reformation. Having accepted a lectureship at the cathedral in Strasburg around 1500, provided by a group of prominent burghers, Kaysersberg constantly referred in his sermons to the need for reform of the clergy as well as an improvement of the laity's lax morals. Similar lectureships were established by wealthy burghers in a number of urban centres in Germany, thus providing employment for outspoken Catholic clergy, independent of the local ecclesiastical hierarchy, willing and able to challenge the shortcomings of the church and its personnel. While demonstrating the vitality of late medieval Catholicism, the criticism of these preachers also stoked the fires of an already growing anticlericalism among the laity.

As you have read in Wallace, the fifteenth century witnessed a dramatic expansion of lay Catholic piety. Perhaps the most important movement for reform inspired by this growing piety was the Brethren of the Common Life, who established themselves in the Netherlands and the neighbouring German Rhineland. The movement became known as the 'modern devotion' and was practised by a semi-monastic but lay brotherhood. Its greatest impact was on higher education, where it affected many prominent figures of the period, including Christian humanists, such as Erasmus of Rotterdam (for Christian humanism see the section below), and the reformer John Calvin, not to mention Martin Luther himself. Luther lived with the Brethren of the Common Life while attending the cathedral school in Magdeburg in 1498 (Beutel, 2003, p. 4). On the popular level, the movement is best remembered by one of its books, *The Imitation of Christ* (1418), a short work that is supposed to have been written by Thomas à Kempis. This proved a highly popular devotional work among both Protestants and Catholics well into the seventeenth century, bridging the confessional divide.

THE SIGNIFICANCE OF CHRISTIAN HUMANISM

You came across the term 'humanism' when you read pp. 67–70 of the set book by Wallace. As Wallace tells us there, 'humanism' was a term invented by nineteenth-century historians rather than by sixteenth-century scholars. Its significance for us in our study of the Reformation is that it played an important role in the thinking of people who came to the conclusion that nothing would do but the reform of the church. Although humanism is sometimes called 'new learning' it would be more accurate to describe it as the rediscovery of ancient texts, mainly in Greek and Latin. It also led to the development of critical textual analysis and to the disciplines of philology, history, poetry and rhetoric, none of which had held much importance in medieval universities, but which came to be more widely applied to all sorts of writing, including the scriptures. Humanism provided the intellectual foundations of reform.

The most famous example of the effect of humanist scholarship was undoubtedly the discovery that the so-called 'Donation of Constantine' was a forgery from the eighth century. It claimed to be a fourth-century grant from Emperor Constantine I, a convert to Christianity, awarding the pope control over the Christian world. No less than three humanist scholars had independently come to the same conclusion, namely that the document was a fake. This was a serious blow to the papal claim to supremacy over the church that rested on this document.

It was not, however, until humanist textual and philological criticism was applied to the Bible that the religious and cultural hegemony of the Catholic Church over early modern society was seriously questioned. As a result, leading Christian humanists came to influence biblical studies and theology. Their influence grew as a result of the learned networks they established, through their correspondence and exchange of manuscripts, and they reached an even wider audience through the newly invented medium of the printing press. Many Christian humanists, such as Heinrich Zwingli (1484–1531) and Philip Melanchthon (1497–1560) became prominent Protestants, but many others, such as Erasmus and John Colet (1467–1519), remained within the Catholic Church. However, Christian humanism undoubtedly prepared the ground for the implementation of religious change generated by the Reformation.

Desiderius Erasmus of Rotterdam (*c.*1467–1536), the most prominent of the Christian humanists, became the leading intellectual light in Europe on the eve of the Reformation. After receiving his schooling in Deventer and 's-Hertogenbosch, while residing with the Brothers of the Common Life, he entered the monastery of the Augustinian Canons at Steyn in 1487, only to escape monastic life five years later. From then on, Erasmus lived a scholarly and itinerant life, spending most of his time in the Netherlands, England and Switzerland. Through his numerous printed publications and his vast correspondence, Erasmus influenced scores of other humanists and later adherents of the Reformation across Europe.

It was Erasmus who proved instrumental in applying humanist scholarship to the Bible. In 1516, he published his New Testament, which contained the original Greek text of the New Testament plus a new Latin translation that differed on many fundamental points from the accepted version used within the Catholic Church – the Vulgate. This, among other things, served to undermine the theological justification for the growing popular devotion to the Virgin Mary, which Erasmus could demonstrate depended on mistranslations and misunderstood biblical allegories. Through his publication of the New Testament, Erasmus set in motion the Reformation debate about whether or not the Bible contained all sacred truth or whether the church could claim to be the guardian of a valid tradition that supplemented the Bible. Erasmus's sarcastic notes on contemporary ecclesiastical practices, and his claim that even if only a very few could be learned, every Christian could be devout and read and understand the Bible on her or his own, proved particularly damaging to the authority of the Catholic Church. It undermined its claims of privilege, special insight and knowledge for its clergy. In this, Erasmus clearly sowed the seeds for some of the more prominent arguments of the evangelical reformers, and here at least there is some truth in the often quoted statement that Erasmus laid the egg Luther hatched.

EXERCISE

Re-read the section 'Humanism, Renaissance and Reformation', in the set book by Wallace, pp. 67–70, and answer the following question:

Does Wallace's interpretation of Christian humanism and Erasmus, and their significance for the Reformation, differ from what you have just read in this unit? If so, how?

Spend about 15 minutes on this exercise.

SPECIMEN ANSWER

There are differences between Wallace and this unit. Wallace emphasises some different aspects of Christian humanism, such as the elitist and intellectual nature of the Christian humanists, and the fact that they wrote in Greek and Latin, not in the vernacular, and therefore could only appeal to a limited audience. He considers Erasmus and the Christian humanists to be detached from the Reformation. He argues that the Christian humanists were not 'inherently reform-oriented nor amenable to the reformation'. Wallace's interpretation emphasises the scholarly approach of the humanists, while arguing that their criticism of the Catholic Church did not amount to a programme for reform. The unit, on the other hand, argues for a much closer relationship and interdependence between Christian humanism and the Reformation.

DISCUSSION

Do not worry that the textbook and the unit are at odds here. This is a good example of how different perspectives on history can result in different interpretations. Hopefully you will have formed your own opinion by the end of the unit.

Erasmus had, however, been critical of Catholic theology and religious institutions long before he published his New Testament. In 1504, he had published his *Enchiridion Militis Christiani* (*The Manual of a Christian Soldier*), which underlined the importance of ordinary laymen studying the Scriptures for themselves. In 1509, he published his stinging satire on monasticism and the corruptions of the church, *Moriae Encomium* (*Praise of Folly*) (the title being a pun on the name of his friend, the humanist Sir Thomas More). This work proved a major bestseller, going through no fewer than seven editions within a few months of its appearance.

EXERCISE

Now read Anthology Document 2.1, 'Erasmus, *The Praise of Folly*, 1511', paragraphs 1–3, and then answer the following two questions:

1   What, according to Folly and Erasmus, was wrong with the religious orders by the beginning of the sixteenth century?

2   Why do you think Erasmus decided to voice his criticism of the church in the form of a satire and through the mouth of Folly, rather than expressing it directly himself?

Spend about 30 minutes on this exercise.

SPECIMEN ANSWER

1   Erasmus has no doubt that the religious orders lacked true piety. Not only were they preoccupied with worldly affairs, but they were also morally corrupt.

2   Erasmus, being a member of the clergy, would have been fully aware of the dangers of being punished and silenced if he chose to express such criticism of the church himself; using Folly served to protect him.

DISCUSSION

1   The monks and friars were, according to Erasmus, more interested in their outward appearances, such as their dress code and the rules of their orders, than in any true, inner religiosity. They were not trying to emulate the spirituality of Christ, as they claimed, but only wanted to compete with each other for the laity's attention and money. In fact, the active begging of many of the mendicant (begging) orders was a public nuisance and detrimental to the truly poor and needy among the local populations – the so-called involuntary poor. Many of the monks and friars were uneducated, even unable to read, and only regurgitated 'by rote the psalms they haven't understood'. Add to that their often amoral and scandalous behaviour, caricatured in the many stories that circulated about debauched, drunken and lecherous monks, and it is no wonder they were, according to Erasmus, universally loathed by the laity. Erasmus also attacked the misuse of power by the mendicant orders in particular, who often made public what they had been told in the confessional, avoiding naming any individuals but providing enough information for the general public to identify the people in question.

2   Apart from demonstrating his humanist credentials by mastering the satire as a literary form, it was, of course, a much safer avenue for a member of the Catholic clergy to take, rather than personally voicing criticism. The use of Folly as his mouthpiece made it far more difficult to link Erasmus with the opinions expressed in the work; accordingly it would have been more difficult to discipline him.

Erasmus remained steadfastly Catholic throughout his life, but his writings were widely attacked by conservative theologians, especially those belonging to the mendicant orders that he had particularly ridiculed. Evidently, his jibe 'monkery is not piety' did little to endear him to the mendicants. He became the target of virulent attacks by Dominicans, Franciscans and Carmelites, who were all opposed to his emphasis on personal Christianity – 'the philosophy of Christ', as he labelled it. Erasmus's theology and tolerance never sat easily with the Catholic Church, and in 1557 the newly created Roman Inquisition sought to ban all his writings by putting them on the Index (a list of prohibited books) (MacCulloch, 2003, p. 277).

A SENSE OF URGENCY: THE SIGNIFICANCE OF APOCALYPTIC EXPECTATIONS FOR THE REFORMATION

As Wallace suggests (pp. 59–60), the expectation of the imminent end of the world and the second coming of Christ were common beliefs in medieval Europe. This was an important reference back to early Christianity: early Christians were exhorted to live each day as if it were their last. The mysterious final book of the New Testament, the Book of Revelation, added support to the idea that there was to be a great cataclysm, that Christ would rule again on earth as a prelude to the end of the world and the Day of Judgement. The Bible, both Old and New Testaments, was used as a text for interpreting past and current events and for checking how far human progress had reached along the path to the Day of Judgement.

Most of the reformers were convinced that they were living in the Last Days and that their actions were part of the unfolding eschatological drama. For them, the Reformation signalled the impending Day of Judgement. Such views were reinforced by the experience of the growing incidence of warfare, famine and disease. This was enhanced by the mounting threat to western Christendom of the expanding Turkish or Ottoman empire, which since the conquest of Constantinople in 1453 had been in control of eastern Christendom, and by the beginning of the sixteenth century was threatening to conquer eastern and central Europe. Without these concerns, and particularly the urgency they generated, the impact of the reformers would undoubtedly have been much slower and less dramatic. The fact that the reformers were able to appropriate the apocalyptic mood of the age for their own propaganda purposes proved crucial. It is impossible to overestimate the value of being able to identify your enemy – the pope and his curia – with Antichrist and his devilish supporters and to make the Reformation part of the last eschatological battle, which people could now read about in the vernacular Bibles translated by the reformers.

It was as a consequence of this that Luther came to be seen not only as a latter day New Testament apostle, but as a prophet. Most often he was portrayed as a second Elijah, who was then identified with one of the two witnesses referred to in Revelation 11; 3–13 – both were sent to identify Antichrist. It is interesting to note that the first portrayal of Luther as a second Elijah came from Heinrich Zwingli, the Swiss reformer in Zurich, whose views on the Reformation did not exactly correspond with Luther's. However, this view of Luther was widely promoted by a variety of people, from Protestant theologians such as Philip Melanchthon (Figure 6.2) to laymen such as the Nuremberg shoemaker Hans Sachs.

Luther himself may have discouraged this identification with Elijah, but he had no doubt that his message of faith and grace was of prophetic importance. Thus he was convinced that the prophecy of the fifteenth-century Franciscan monk Johann Hilten, which predicted the rise of a godly reformer in 1516 who would reform the church, referred to him personally. Likewise, Luther was

Figure 6.2   Lucas Cranach, the Younger, *Philip Melanchthon*, 1560, woodcut, Berlin. Photo: AKG-Images, London

convinced that the prediction of John Hus (*c.*1372–1415), which Hus was supposed to have made shortly before being burnt as a heretic, pointed to him. Luther therefore claimed:

> Holy Johannes Hus prophesyed about me when he wrote from his Bohemian prison that they might now be roasting a goose (for Hus means goose), but in a hundred years they will hear a swan sing, which they will not be able to silence.

> (Cunnigham and Grell, 2000, p. 25)

Figure 6.3 Albrecht Dürer, *Frederick the Wise of Saxony*, 1524 copperplate engraving, 18.8 x 12.2 cm. Photo: AKG-Images, London

Linked to these apocalyptic expectations about the appearance of a great prophet was another medieval prophecy, the so-called Sibylline Oracles, about the advent of a last emperor, who would reform both the Holy Roman Empire and the church before the Last Judgement. Occasionally, this prophecy served to advocate social and political reforms too. Mainly, however, it took the form of a prediction that a new emperor, a third Frederick, a successor to Frederick II, would take on the papacy and reform Christianity, preparing the way for Christ's second coming. Many pamphleteers, including Luther, identified this Frederick with Luther's protector Frederick the Wise of Saxony (Figure 6.3).

Luther undoubtedly saw life on earth as engulfed in the never-ending conflict between God and the Devil from which there was no escape. He had no doubt that he was living through the Last Days and that the Gospel of St Matthew applied to his own time. Already in 1514 he was convinced that 'the Gospel of St Matthew counts such perversions as the sale of indulgencies among the signs of the End of the World'. In 1522, Luther chose the signs of the second coming of Christ as his subject of an Advent sermon:

> I would compel no man to believe me, and yet in this manner I will not yield up my Judgement to any other, namely, that the Last Day is not farr off ... Let us not therefore be wanting to ourselves, disregarding the most diligent premonition and prophecie of Christ our Saviour; but seeing in our Age the Signs foretold by him, do often come to pass, let us not think that the coming of Christ is far off. [...]

> Besides, we have seen not a few Comets, having the form of the Cross, imprinted from heaven, both on the bodies and garments of men, new kind of diseases, as the French Pox, and some others. How many other signs also, and unusual impressions, have we seen in the Heavens, in the Sun, Moon, Stars, rain-bows and strange Apparitions in these last four years?
>
> (Cunningham and Grell, 2000, pp. 26, 73)

EXERCISE Having read the section above, how, in your opinion, did Luther reach his conviction that the end of the world was imminent?

Spend about 10 minutes on this exercise.

SPECIMEN ANSWER Through his study of the Bible, Luther had become convinced that the Day of Judgement was close. Christians were obliged to take Christ's prophesies seriously and to look for confirmation in the natural world that the Last Day was imminent. This included the many astrological phenomena that had been seen over the previous four years, not to mention the arrival of new diseases.

Luther's identification of the papacy with Antichrist turned out to be the most important of all his biblical prophetic 'discoveries', and had the greatest significance for the apocalyptic mood of the times and for promoting Luther's programme of religious reform. The appearance of Antichrist was intimately linked to the Last Days in the Bible as well as in Christian tradition. The ambivalence of the figure of Antichrist only enhanced his legendary qualities, as did the vague scheme of eschatological events attached to his defeat. He had already been identified with the pope by earlier critics of the church, such as John Hus. Their claims, however, had been founded on moral grounds, such as the worldliness and depravity of the pope and his cardinals. Luther's indictment was based on doctrine and principle. For Luther, reforming the church was not about improving its ethics, but about the urgent and fundamental need to salvage the Word of God from the agents of the Devil before it was too late. Luther made this 'discovery' as early as 1518, but did not develop it fully until his major publications in 1520, which you will encounter in the next section of this unit.

The full propaganda value of this 'discovery' was quickly used by Luther's friend, the court painter and publicist Lucas Cranach, the Elder, who, like Luther, resided in Wittenberg. In 1521, Cranach published a small illustrated pamphlet, *Passional Christi und Antichristi*, containing twenty-six woodcuts, each with a brief comment by Luther's friend and colleague Philip Melanchthon. The impact of this work, which juxtaposed the life and actions of Antichrist, clearly identifiable with the pope, with those of Christ, can hardly be exaggerated. Not only did it run through a number of editions within a few years, but it also came to shape and direct the evangelical, antipapal propaganda for decades to come.

The twelfth set of Cranach's woodcuts for this pamphlet provides a good example of how this propaganda worked (see the *Visual Sources Book,* Plate 5.1). To the right we see Christ driving the money-changers out of the temple. To the left this is contrasted with Antichrist, sitting on the papal throne wearing the papal tiara, surrounded by cardinals and bishops selling indulgences (documents remitting sins). The text underneath the illustrations confirms this interpretation with direct biblical evidence. It points out that it has all been foretold in the Book of Daniel, where we are told that Antichrist will alter divine ordinances, suppress Holy Scripture, and sell dispensations, indulgences, palliums and bishoprics (Scribner, 1994, pp. 153–4).

| EXERCISE | Now look closely at Plate 5.2 in the *Visual Sources Book*, which shows a broadsheet entitled *About the Origin of the Monks. About the Origin of Antichrist*, and answer the following questions: |

1   Give a description of this broadsheet.

2   What is the message?

Spend about 15 minutes on this exercise.

| SPECIMEN ANSWER | 1   It shows devils defecating monks, who are then collected by other devils and put into a mortar, where they are mashed up to create the raw material from which the devils construct Antichrist. Antichrist is shown wearing a papal tiara, making the identification of the pope with Antichrist unmistakable. |

2   The message is simple: monastic orders are the Devil's invention while the pope, another construction by the Devil, is Antichrist.

MARTIN LUTHER AND THE BEGINNING OF THE REFORMATION

<table>
<tr>
<td>

EXERCISE

</td>
<td>

Re-read the section entitled 'Luther as Reformer' in the set book by Wallace, pp. 75–81. Use what you have read to answer the following two questions:

1   Did Luther, in your opinion, have a fully developed Protestant programme for reform when he pinned his ninety-five theses against indulgences onto the church door of the Castle Church in Wittenberg on 31 October 1517?

2   Describe Luther's new concept of faith.

Spend about 20 minutes on this exercise.

</td>
</tr>
<tr>
<td>

SPECIMEN ANSWER

</td>
<td>

1   No.

2   Justification by faith alone – nothing else mattered.

</td>
</tr>
<tr>
<td>

DISCUSSION

</td>
<td>

1   It was only by the end of 1520 that Luther had developed the three major platforms of his evangelical theology, namely: justification by faith alone, the sole authority of Scripture, and the priesthood of all believers.

2   Is was undoubtedly through his lecturers on the epistles of Paul, which he had begun at the University of Wittenberg in 1513, that Luther came to believe that man could do nothing to secure his salvation, either by himself or through the mediation of the Catholic Church in the form of pious acts. Faith in God's mercy and love was all that was required.

</td>
</tr>
</table>

So what was the significance of Luther's ninety-five theses? Their attack on the selling of letters of indulgence by the church, whereby the purchaser bought him/herself remission of sins and a speedier journey through purgatory clearly found popular resonance, and news of their publication spread rapidly across Germany and beyond. The theses quickly appeared in print. They can be said to represent the first step towards what eventually became the Reformation. By publishing his theses, Luther not only challenged the claims of the indulgence preachers that they were able to remit sins, but he also questioned the authority of the pope to do the same. Little, however, could Luther have known, or for that matter intended, that this would be the beginning of the European Reformation. Even later, while the unity of the church was dissolving around him with increasing speed, Luther continued to claim that none of this was due to him: 'While I slept or drank Wittenberg beer ... the Word so greatly weakened the papacy that never a Prince or Emperor inflicted such damage upon it. I did nothing, the Word did it all' (Collinson, 2003, p. 17). By making the Bible available for all Germans in the vernacular while emphasising it as the sole authority in matters of faith, Luther not only created problems for the pope, but eventually also for himself. As we shall see below, not everyone came to the same conclusions as Luther about what truth the Bible revealed.

Martin Luther (1483–1546) (see Figure 6.4) was the first and most prominent of the early reformers. Luther had enjoyed a successful academic vocation, obtaining both his BA and his MA from the University of Erfurt, while simultaneously receiving ordination and becoming an Augustinian monk, before his transfer to the new University in Wittenberg in 1511. Six years later, his posting of the ninety-five theses in Wittenberg started him off on the course that would lead to the Reformation. By 1518, Luther had already become a prominent figure in Germany – a trial for heresy against him began in Rome during the summer and without the support of his territorial ruler, Elector Frederick the Wise of Saxony, Luther would undoubtedly have been excommunicated by the end of 1518, followed by the ban of the empire. Instead, he came through the interrogation of the papal legate, Cajetan, at the Diet of Augsburg in October 1518, and the theological debate with Johann Eck, the Ingolstadt professor of theology in the summer of 1519 in Leipzig. Not until 15 June 1520 was a bill threatening Luther with excommunication issued from Rome. Still Frederick the Wise was able to protect him and secure him a hearing at the Diet of Worms in April 1521. This was largely due to the central role of the elector of Saxony in the forthcoming election of a new Holy Roman Emperor, where both the Habsburgs and the Roman curia badly needed his support. Luther's activities as a preacher, university teacher, writer and translator proved of paramount importance for the success of the Reformation.

The protection offered him by Elector Frederick the Wise of Saxony provided Luther with a window of opportunity. This allowed him not only to develop his criticism of the Catholic Church and the pope (challenging the infallibility of the pope and church councils) while formulating his own theology, but also to widen his appeal through a number of important publications. Luther published no less than four major tracts in 1520, all of which achieved wide circulations and were published in numerous editions. First published was the tract *Of Good Works* (1520), in which Luther claimed that faith alone was enough to fulfil the ten commandments and that good works did not contribute to salvation; in fact, truly good works only followed from a life lived in faith and grace.

Then followed the hugely influential *To the Christian Nobility of the German Nation* (1520), in which Luther encouraged the German princes to use their rights as secular authorities actively to support the reform of Christianity. Written in German, and primarily aimed at the laity, it sold like hot cakes. Within a few days of its appearance, its first print-run of 4,000 copies had sold out and a second, larger edition was being prepared for the press. Shortly afterwards, the Latin pamphlet *On the Babylonian Captivity of the Church* (1520) appeared. This work was geared towards a theologically educated market – hence the choice of Latin. Here Luther rejected four of the seven Catholic sacraments (Confirmation, Marriage, Ordination and Extreme Unction) as human invention, while also voicing some reservations about the sacrament of Repentance as being unbiblical. Only two sacraments were,

Figure 6.4 Lucas Cranach, the Younger, *Martin Luther, c.*1546, woodcut, Berlin. Germanisches Nationalmuseum, Nuremberg, Inv.-Nr. H7400. Photo: Germanisches Nationalmuseum

Figure 6.5   Lucas Cranach, the Elder, *The Lutheran service*, 1520s. Note that the Eucharist is given in both forms – wine and bread – to the laity, while the Catholic clergy is swallowed by the monster of Hell. Photo: Warburg Institute, London

according to Luther, instituted by Scripture, namely Baptism and the Eucharist. No distinction should be made between laity and clergy with regard to the Eucharist – everyone should receive it in both forms: bread and wine. Luther also took the opportunity to criticise the Catholic Church's understanding of the Mass and the Eucharist (see Figure 6.5). This was, according to Luther, based on the false notion that a special priesthood existed, and that the Mass was a sacrifice. According to the New Testament, the priestly office was one of preaching and could be undertaken by all Christians, and was not an office for making sacrifices. This was explosive stuff, which removed the clergy's claim to special status. Erasmus, who so far had supported Luther, recognised the significance of this pamphlet when stating that the chances of a compromise with the Roman curia had now evaporated.

Finally, the tract *On the Freedom of a Christian* (1520) was published. In it, Luther argued that faith in God and God's freely granted grace released Christians from the necessity for self-justification before God, liberating them to show compassion and love of their neighbours in their commitment to their families and local communities.

EXERCISE

Now read Anthology Document 2.2, 'Martin Luther, *To the Christian Nobility of the German Nation*, 1520', and then answer the following questions:

1   Who was Luther's primary audience for this tract?

2   What were the obstacles, according to Luther, that had hitherto prevented reform of the church?

3   Who had created the 'spiritual estate' and why?

Spend about 25 minutes on this exercise.

1   Luther did not, as the title seems to indicate, aim his pamphlet primarily at the German nobility or the territorial princes in Germany, but addressed it in particular to the emperor.

2   It was, according to Luther, the pope and the curia that had prevented reform.

3   Luther had no doubt that this was an invention of the Catholic Church, done solely to protect the interests of the clergy.

1   Luther was directing *To the Christian Nobility of the German Nation* primarily at the newly elected Emperor Charles V (Figure 6.6), who had become Holy Roman Emperor in 1519 at the age of twenty, and the German territorial princes, included under the heading 'Christian nobility'. It is noteworthy that, at this stage, Luther still hoped that Charles V, together with the territorial princes, might undertake a reformation of the church.

2   According to Luther, the Roman curia had prevented all attempts at reform by claiming: first, that temporal power held no jurisdiction over them, and that they – the spiritual power – took precedence; second, that any attempts at reform had failed and were doomed to fail, even when firmly based in Scripture, due to the pope's claim that only he could interpret Scripture; third, that all councils of the church had failed in their attempts to reform the church, because the popes claimed that only they could call councils. Furthermore, when councils were called, the popes always managed to manipulate the princes to take no action while making sure that they maintained full control over the execution of the decisions of the councils.

3   The 'spiritual estate' was an invention of the church and, according to Luther, it had been invented solely to support clerical privileges and power. It therefore had no scriptural foundation. Quoting Paul, Luther stated that there was no difference between men except that of their office or occupation whereby human beings served each other and the community they lived in. There was, in other words, no qualitative difference between a blacksmith and a priest: both served the same community in a different capacity.

Luther's hope of convincing Emperor Charles V of the need for reform of the church proved futile. Despite his excommunication in October 1520, Luther remained a free man protected by Frederick the Wise, who also managed to secure him a hearing with the promise of safe conduct at the Diet of Worms in April 1521. Here Luther, facing the emperor and the imperial estates, refused to recant, arguing that his conscience was tied by Holy Scripture.

From then on, Luther was not only excommunicated by the church, but the Edict of Worms placed him under the imperial ban, which made it legal for anyone to kill him. His life was thus in real danger and all his books and publications were to be burnt across the empire. It was in order to guarantee

Figure 6.6 Christoph Amberger, *Emperor Charles V*, *c*.1530, woodcut, 42.6 x 26.4 cm. Photo: AKG-Images, London

his safety that Frederick the Wise had Luther, who was on his way back to Wittenberg, picked up by soldiers and taken to Wartburg Castle.

Luther's ability to write for and communicate with the common people proved of tremendous significance. His German pamphlets were able to convey his message in an extremely entertaining and clear form, thereby securing a wide readership. His sermons and lectures held a similar popular appeal. Considering his many engagements and written works, it is impressive that Luther continued to preach and lecture regularly. It is important to remember that the sermon, which had become increasingly significant during the late fifteenth century, became perhaps the most important vehicle by which reformers spread their message and promoted their theology.

That all the evangelical reformers wrote in the vernacular and many were engaged in translating the Bible into their national languages proved of paramount importance for spreading their message and their claim that their faith was based on the pure Word of God. Most of these translations also proved to be major landmarks in the development of national languages in Protestant countries, such as Luther's Bible for Germany, William Tyndale's New Testament and Miles Coverdale's Bible for England, John Calvin's Bible for France, and Peder Palladius's Bible for Denmark.

However, Luther was disappointed in his hope that the secular rulers would provide unqualified support for his cause and help reform the church. Even the territorial princes who were later to support the Reformation refrained from giving Luther any support at this stage. Instead, reforms were first introduced locally by individual towns in electoral Saxony and some imperial cities, starting with Nuremberg and Strasburg. Meanwhile, however, the evangelical message spread rapidly and gained increasing support at the popular level.

Despite the immediate popular appeal of Luther's ideas, it took time for the new evangelical ideas to influence governments and princes, both within and outside the Holy Roman Empire. Gradually, however, during the 1520s the evangelical faith gained new adherents among the princes and rulers of Europe and it began to influence contemporary political thinking and views on the role and shape of the state.

FROM REFORM TO REVOLT

The momentum for reform gathered pace at grass-roots level, and what Luther had set in motion proved impossible to stop or, for that matter, to control. Not only was another and somewhat different reformer, Heinrich Zwingli, making a significant impact in Zurich in Switzerland and the southern parts of Germany, but other former allies of Luther, such as Andreas Karlstadt (c.1480–1541) and Thomas Müntzer (c.1489–1525), were radicalising Luther's suggestions for reforms and taking them beyond what he had intended. Everyone agreed with Luther that reforms of the church were urgently needed, but when it came to what form they should take there was little consensus. Groups with political and social grievances found support for their causes in

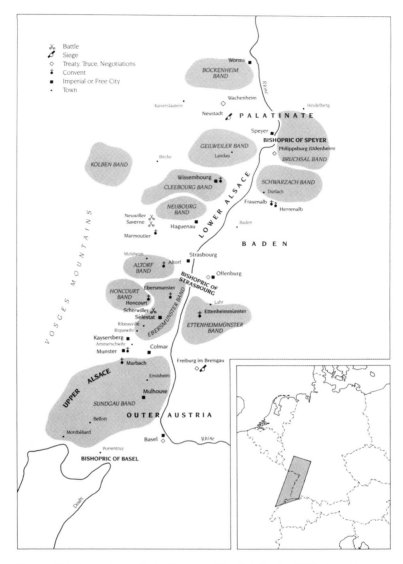

Figure 6.7   Peasant revolts in Alsace and the Palatinate, 1525, from Tom Scott and Bob Scribner (1991) *The German Peasants' War*, New Jersey and London: Humanities Press International Inc., pp. 46–7

Luther's ideas. Thus, the support that Luther gained from the imperial knights already proved a liability towards the end of 1522, when their armed rebellion was suppressed by a group of territorial princes. Likewise, the claim of the peasants to have evangelical and scriptural justification for their rebellion (the so-called Peasants' War of 1524–25) alarmed Luther and in his opinion only served to endanger the prospects of a real reformation.

The Peasants' War began in the summer of 1524 in the southern Black Forest and then spread rapidly to many areas of south-western Germany and Switzerland by April and May 1525 (see Figure 6.7). These were regions that had witnessed peasant unrest before, but this time their cause was actively supported by many urban communities, ranging from small rural towns to some larger cities. The scale of the rebellion was considerable and the rebels were well organised and supported by seasoned troops. It has been estimated that, when they were defeated in June 1525, between 70,000 and 100,000 people (mainly rebels) had lost their lives.

EXERCISE	To help you understand what Anabaptists and so-called radicals believed, read the set book by Wallace, pp. 82–9.

Spend about 10 minutes on this exercise.

DISCUSSION	From your reading of Wallace, you will realise the importance of religion and evangelical preachers such as Thomas Müntzer for the revolt. The rebels justified active resistance and alternative forms of government with reference to the Bible.

Thomas Müntzer, who had been inspired by Luther to join the evangelical party, quickly came to believe in a more radical approach to reform in which the godly were obliged to bring about religious reform with force if necessary. He had also come to see his own ministry as prophetic and expected the end of the world to be imminent. Together with a number of other radical evangelicals, such as the so-called Zwickau prophets, he saw it as his and other godly people's obligation to help bring about the second coming of Christ by taking up arms against those who opposed the Gospel (see Figure 6.8). Müntzer's call to arms in order to hasten the end of the world and bring about a just kingdom of God, not surprisingly, failed to gain the support of the German evangelical princes, but it did gain considerable support and popularity among the rebellious peasants and their associates in southern Germany, many of whom found further justification for their cause in Müntzer's chiliastic interpretation of the Gospel. On the eve of the outbreak of the Peasants' War in the spring of 1524, Müntzer wrote to his supporters in the town of Eisenach. Quoting Daniel 7, he stated that 'the kingdom and the dominion and the greatness of the kingdoms under the whole heaven shall be given to the people of the saints of the Most High; their kingdom shall be an everlasting kingdom, and all dominions shall serve and obey them'. Müntzer then pointed out that the 'common man' was to rule this kingdom until Christ's second coming. God's prophet Thomas Müntzer presented his followers with a simple choice – either they sided with him and God and took militant action or they were with the Devil and against him. Müntzer signed this and many of his last letters 'Thomas Müntzer with the sword of Gideon'. Thus, it was as a second Gideon – a defeater of false beliefs and of the enemies of God's people – that Müntzer took up arms and joined the peasants' forces in the battle of Frankenhausen in May 1525 (Cunningham and Grell, 2000, p. 33).

As you have read in Wallace, it was the worsening economic climate in south-west Germany, with rising prices and the attempts by feudal lords to extract higher fees and more services from their tenants, that caused peasants and artisans to rebel. The peasants rebellion, in other words, does not only

Figure 6.8   Erhard Schön, *Prophecy about the Peasants' War,* 1523, woodcut. Photo: AKG-Images, London

illustrate the significance of the module theme of beliefs and ideologies, but also the theme of producers and consumers, here represented by peasants and feudal lords.

The rebels were accused by those in authority of 'turning Swiss' – a reference to the Swiss Confederacy, which had no feudal lords and was seen to be ruled by the 'common man'. The rebels' aims and ambitions differed from locality to locality, reflecting local issues. However, the Twelve Articles set down in the upper Swabian town of Memmingen managed to attract wide consent from the rebels. They had been written with considerable input of the local evangelical ministers. The articles were immediately widely copied by other rebels, printed, read and discussed over and over again in the many peasant armies.

EXERCISE

Read Anthology Document 2.3, 'The Twelve Articles of the Upper Swabian peasants, February 1525', and answer the following questions:

1 What, according to the peasants, is the ultimate yardstick for their demands?

2 Who shall be in control of their churches?

3 What are the peasants' main demands?

Spend about 25 minutes on this exercise.

SPECIMEN ANSWER

1 The Word of God (i.e. the Bible).

2 The peasants themselves.

3 Freedom and the acknowledgement of their ancient rights.

DISCUSSION

1 The peasants claim that their demands are all in accordance with the Gospel. This is made clear in the last of the Twelve Articles, in which they declare that they will withdraw any demand that is against the Word of God or can be seen as 'improper' according to it. They also demand pastors for their communities who preach the Word of God (i.e. evangelical preachers), and they insist that they are released from their feudal obligations, which they consider to be against Scripture. They are, in other words, demanding that Scripture becomes the yardstick of all political and social life.

2 The peasants want an evangelical church, where the power rests solely with the individual congregation, who should be able to elect and remove their own pastors. The emphasis is on a congregational model, where powers rest with the whole community. Elected churchwardens should collect the tithe, but only in the form of a grain tithe, which, according to the peasants, is the only tithe that is in accordance with the Bible. The churchwardens should then pay the parson enough to support himself and his family, but the level of pay should be decided by the whole congregation. What is left should then be spent on the poor.

3 The peasants' first political demand in the articles is to have their serfdom removed. They demand to be treated as free Christians, justifying their demand with reference to the Gospel. They want the right to hunt and fish in rivers and streams, again with reference to the Bible, and demand that all woods should be considered communal land. They also demand a fairer treatment by their lords, such as just rents, not to mention better pay for their services. They want a stop

to new laws being issued and used against them and a restoration of their ancient rights, especially where fields and meadows belonging to the community have been taken over by local lords.

It is noteworthy that this rebellion of peasants and artisans never questioned individual rights of ownership and that they primarily aimed to reduce the economic burden placed on them. The rebels wanted to create a more egalitarian social order. To apply the term 'revolutionary' to them would be a mistake; the movement remained too diffuse and limited in its objectives. That does not mean, however, that revolutionary events did not occur, as when men and women stormed local monasteries, demonstrating their long pent-up anger against the privileged existence of monks and nuns, whose 'wasteful' lives had become a special target for the evangelical movement. Later, peasant women near Heggbach convent, which had been plundered by their husbands, even threatened the nuns there with having their eyes scratched out and with rape if they did not refrain from pursuing their men for the plunder of the convent's goods (Rublack, 2005, p. 28).

In the period leading up to the Peasants' War, there had already been disturbances in many Alsatian cities where evangelical demands for reform had merged with social grievances. Early in 1525, there had been an anticlerical revolt in Saverne, the residence of the bishop of Strasburg, while several villages under the rule of the city of Strasburg had demanded the appointment of evangelical preachers. On 2 April 1525, armed peasants had assembled in the village of Heiligenstein to free the Strasburg gardener and radical preacher Clemens Ziegler, who had been imprisoned for unauthorised evangelical preaching. Despite managing to have Ziegler released, more peasants took up arms and a fortnight later a band of rebels had formed and a committee elected with Erasmus Gerber, who was to prove one of the most prominent of the peasants' leaders, as its head and spokesman. Gerber, who clearly had military experience, organised the Alsatian bands along the lines of the territorial militia. The following day, Gerber's band accepted the Twelve Articles and a force of 400 peasants occupied the abbey of Altorf. On 17 April, Gerber invited the evangelical preachers from Strasburg to come to Altorf, asking them to acknowledge their cause as Christian and to mediate a settlement. The three leading Strasburg preachers, Wolfgang Capito, Matthias Zell and Martin Bucer, were enthusiastically received by the peasants and responded in writing on their way back to Strasburg.

<table>
<tr><td>EXERCISE</td><td>Read Anthology Document 2.4, 'Strasbourg preachers' reply to the Alsatian peasants, 18 April 1525', and answer the following questions:

1   What do the preachers advise the peasants to do?

2   What are their reasons for giving the peasants their advice?

Spend about 20 minutes on this exercise.</td></tr>
</table>

SPECIMEN ANSWER

1   Accept the proposal of the mediators appointed by the Strasburg council (Sir Martin Herlin and Lord Bernhard Ottfriedrich).

2   The peasants are acting against their own best interests and against the Gospel by taking up arms.

DISCUSSION

1   The Strasburg preachers start their letter by emphasising their sympathy for the peasants' cause, pointing out that they have always tried to 'lighten the burdens upon the common man'. They claim to have the peasants' best interests at heart when they advise the peasants to accept the proposal of the mediators appointed by the Strasburg council: namely to disband in exchange for no reprisals being taken against them for having taken up arms, and to wait for the outcome of the negotiations about the Twelve Articles.

2   The preachers' response falls into parts. The first eight points address the military and political dangers to the peasants if they refuse to disband and return home. First, the larger their forces become, the more difficulties they will encounter in finding the provisions they need. Second, provisions are likely to run out long before negotiations about the Twelve Articles will have been concluded. Third, a larger force does not offer greater security for the peasants, as can be seen from the example of the Swabian peasants (the point refers to their recent defeats). Fourth, by continuing their uprising, the peasants may antagonise those who are still sympathetic to their cause. Fifth, the support and sympathy of the city of Strasburg might be squandered if the rebellion is continued. Points 10–13 address the religious reasons why the peasants should disarm and return home. Here the preachers emphasise that it is contrary to the Gospel for the rebels not to accept the proposal of the mediators, and that nowhere in the Bible can support be found for the killing of an unjust ruler. They also warn the peasants about seeking their own ends under the pretext of the Gospel. If they do so, they would be severely punished by God. The preachers conclude that, as Christians, the peasants should seek peace and desire God's honour not their own.

The evangelical justification for their uprising was important to the Alsatian peasants and artisans, and many of their banners carried evangelical symbols and inscriptions, such as 'Jesus Christ' and 'The Word of God will stand forever'. They gained no serious support from any of the major Alsatian towns, although internal unrest was generated by groups sympathetic to the rebels' cause. Here, as elsewhere, the social composition of the rebels was far from being exclusively rural. This, in turn, may well have made it difficult for urban magistrates to take firm action against the rebels.

The Alsatian peasant rebellion proved short-lived. The peasant bands were soundly defeated by the duke of Lorraine the following month. On 16 May, the peasants, who had resisted the duke's siege of Saverne, surrendered. The whole affair came to a gruesome conclusion when the peasants marching unarmed out of the town were massacred by the duke's mercenaries – several thousand were slaughtered. Their leader, Erasmus Gerber was apprehended and hanged the following day in Saverne.

PRINT, IMAGE AND THE SPOKEN WORD: GETTING THE MESSAGE ACROSS

The activities of the Christian humanists and the evangelical reformers who inspired and instigated the Reformation followed closely on the invention of printing, which opened up the potential for mass communication. By the sixteenth century, affordable printed books were for the first time available to ordinary people who could read. If the humanists made good use of printing to engage with the scholarly and educated elite across Europe, it was the evangelical reformers who realised the potential of the printing press as a mass medium. Martin Luther considered printing to be 'God's highest and extremest act of grace, by which the business of the Gospel is driven forward'. Similarly, the Protestant author of *Actes and Monuments* (*The Book of Martyrs*), John Foxe, expressed the view that 'God has opened the press to preach, whose voice the Pope is never able to stop with all the puissance of his triple crown'. Consequently, the Reformation led to a publication explosion (Cunnigham and Grell, 2000, p. 17).

The beginning of the sixteenth century also turned out to be the first time in history that illustrative material, in the form of woodcuts, became widely available at affordable prices. A considerable proportion of these illustrations appeared as single-leaf broadsheets, often incorporating an explanatory text in prose or verse. Today we describe the use of email and the web as an 'information revolution'. The same term could just as well be used to describe what happened in the sixteenth century, when books, small and large, and illustrated broadsheets suddenly became widely available. Being a hybrid form of image and text, and given the nature of reading in the period, when texts were often read aloud, the broadsheets combined text and image with oral communication, and were aimed at the literate and illiterate mass market. It proved a highly efficient mode of propaganda for Protestants in particular, as you have already seen in this unit.

Erasmus, in his criticism of the clergy and monasticism, had added fuel to the popular, and growing, late medieval anticlericalism. On the eve of the Reformation, this anticlericalism had already been targeting monks and friars for some time in a number of critical and satirical broadsheets attacking the moral and religious shortfalls of the monastic orders. In this respect, the reformers only took up a well-established tradition, while stoking the flames by pointing out that these orders, with their emphasis on celibacy, voluntary poverty and a contemplative life, had no place in an evangelical church.

A good example of such a broadsheet from the early 1520s is shown in the *Visual Sources Book*, Plate 5.3. This broadsheet also attacked the economic activities of the monastic orders by depicting the monk as a spoon-maker/seller. Because the clergy enjoyed exemption from paying tax, by the beginning of the sixteenth century their economic activities were increasingly being perceived as detrimental to the laity. At the same time, this broadsheet presents monasticism as 'spoon-work' – a sixteenth century allegory for doing something of little use or consequence. The woodcut, however, would not be comprehensible without the text included in the seven scrolls spread around the edge of the picture. The scroll in the top left-hand corner points out that it is a disgrace that monks have become spoon-sellers. The scroll placed sideways to the left gives voice to the larger monk's thoughts. He complains that monasticism is nothing but useless spoon-work. Had he known this, he would never have entered his order, but instead he would have studied so that he could become a credit to God and society. This scroll could have been taken straight out of Erasmus. The small monk collecting spoons from the ground voices similar concerns in the scroll directly below him. Since he has to undertake such menial and useless tasks, as a junior member of the order (also indicated by his smaller size), he has decided to put up his spoons (i.e. leave the order).

The scroll in the top centre contains another complaint from the larger monk: monasticism is in low regard – in fact, his order is held in such low regard that even the old woman in the picture is scolding him. She is identified as a miller's wife in the scroll in the bottom right-hand corner. She reproves him for his idle life and threatens to 'pick off his lice' with her spoon, which she has evidently broken in the process. The old woman adds to her criticism of the monk with her statement in the scroll in the top right-hand corner. He should have kept to his books and he should do something about his pox, before the flies (large specimens of which can be seen in the woodcut) eat him and turn him into a shadow. This alludes to the sexual amorality often associated with monks in the period. The sexual connotation of this accusation is further enhanced by the last scroll on the right-hand side of the broadsheet, where the old woman asks the monk: 'What are you gawping at, look rather at the ape's arsehole'. Here she is clearly referring to the ape in the woodcut, showing his back-side to the monk, while inquiring: Do you know the old ape of Heidelberg? This is a reference to the figure of an ape that stood on the stone bridge in Heidelberg bearing the inscription: 'Why do you gawp at me, have you never seen an old ape? Look around Heidelberg and you will find many more'. This was, of course, originally intended to point out the folly of academic life, but used here it was transferred to monasticism. At the same time, it also echoed Luther's views of monasticism as an 'ape's and fool's game' (Scribner, 1994, pp. 41–2).

EXERCISE

Now look at Figure 6.9, a broadsheet by Hans Sebald Beham entitled 'Allegory of monastic orders', and answer the following question:

What does this image seek to tell us about the monastic orders?

(The Latin titles given to the three female characters to the left of the picture signify the vices of Pride (Superbia), Luxury and Lust (Luxuria), and Greed (Avaricia). That to the right of the picture signifies the virtue of Poverty (Paupertas).

Spend about 15 minutes on this exercise.

Figure 6.9 Hans Sebald Beham, *Allegory of monastic orders*, 1521, wood engraving, Vienna. Photo: The Warburg Institute, London

SPECIMEN ANSWER

The image tells us that the monastic orders are corrupt and only interested in their own gain.

DISCUSSION

The centre of the image shows a friar being held back and controlled by the vices of Pride, Luxury and Greed, who have a scarf around his neck. This represents the exact opposite of what holy orders and monasticism claimed to be all about. The friar, who represents the voluntary poor (those who have opted for a life in poverty to serve Christ), is being confronted by a poor man in rags, representing the rightful involuntary poor, whom the friar should have cared for in the first instance. He grips the friar by his forelock, forcing him to eat a book while being encouraged in his action by Poverty. Clearly, the friar has wrongfully encroached on the charity that should rightfully go to the involuntary poor and is now being forced to eat either the rule book of his order or the Word of God. It is a strongly anticlerical message.

The fact, however, that the evangelical reformers, and Luther in particular, were able to make good use of the already prevailing anticlericalism in their propaganda against the Catholic Church does not explain the speed with which the evangelical message and Luther's religious views were spread. Some historians have tended to see the success of the Reformation as a result of the printing revolution. For the first time in history it had become possible to mass produce books and pamphlets, thereby making it possible to reach the mass market of potential consumers with a product they could afford. Evidently, the printing and sale of cheap pamphlets proved nearly impossible to control for the authorities, be they lay or ecclesiastical, while Luther's writings proved popular, not least because they articulated long-standing complaints about the church while giving them new and explosive theological justification. Focusing exclusively on the significance of printing – which was, after all, only the medium – tends to overlook the significance of Luther's message. In contrast to those who had criticised the church before him, such as the Bohemian John Hus, with whom Luther felt a close affiliation, who had all attacked the external abuses of the church, Luther was the first to attack what he perceived to be the corrupt theology of the church based on what he claimed to be the true Word of God – the Gospel. To quote Patrick Collinson:

> Luther, who liked a pungent phrase, would have been glad to agree that only he had gone for the jugular. And here we can propose a nice paradox: whereas a century of talk about reform had been no more than that, mere words on paper, Luther's single-minded concentration on the Word brought about real and revolutionary change.
>
> (Collinson, 2003, pp. 24–5)

THE SIGNIFICANCE OF WITTENBERG

But the evangelical message still had to be disseminated, and in this connection the place Luther operated from is significant. Wittenberg (see the *Visual Sources Book*, Plate 5.4), where Luther arrived in 1511 as a member of the recently founded Augustinian monastery, was not a large town by any standards. It consisted of 400 houses and had around 2,000 inhabitants. Compared with cities such as Strasburg and Nuremberg, which had around 20,000 and 40,000 inhabitants, respectively, it was an insignificant place. One would expect its lack of size and consequence to have hampered the spread of Luther's evangelical ideas. But it is more than likely that Wittenberg's insignificance proved an advantage for Luther and his supporters. Compared with larger cities, it had far fewer civic institutions and different interest groups – its citizens were largely artisans who served the local market – who needed to be satisfied and won over to the Reformation.

Furthermore, the fact that Wittenberg had recently become a seat of residence for the dukes of electoral Saxony (Saxony had been divided between two brothers, Ernst and Albrecht, in 1485) and acquired a university proved an added advantage for the success of the Reformation. Ernst's son Frederick the Wise, who ruled electoral Saxony from 1486 to 1525, invested heavily in Wittenberg. He founded the university in 1502 and attracted some of the finest artists to his court in Wittenberg, among them Lucas Cranach, the Elder. He corresponded with prominent humanists, collected books and, more surprisingly for someone who was to provide strong backing for Luther and the evangelical cause, he became an avid collector of relics, which he exhibited once a year.

All this helped to put Wittenberg on the map, attracting visitors, students, professors and new inhabitants. Wittenberg, with its many new buildings and university, offered new opportunities to the young and ambitious, but most importantly it had few traditions and vested interests to hinder innovation.

Luther, who began lecturing in biblical studies at the university in 1513, became increasingly influential within the new university. He was able to influence not only the curriculum, but also new appointments, such as that of Philip Melanchthon, who became his close collaborator in promoting the Reformation, as initially did his university colleague Andreas Karlstadt. Only a small new university would have made this possible. Luther, of course, could also rely on the support of Frederick the Wise through his excellent relations with the duke's secretary, Georg Spalatin. Accordingly, Wittenberg in the wake of the publication of the ninety-five theses in 1517 acquired a reputation for innovation; it rejected the traditional Aristotelian and scholastic approach to university learning while emphasising the importance of Biblical exegesis for establishing Biblical truth as the basis for Luther's doctrine of grace. This resulted in a dramatic rise in the number of students who attended the University of Wittenberg after 1517.

Increasingly, students from all over Germany and Europe were attracted to Wittenberg to encounter these young university professors, who were all in their thirties and who wanted to reform the church. Apart from attending the lectures given by Luther and Melanchthon, many of these students also boarded with their teachers and became closely attached to them. Some, like Johannes Bugenhagen, became close collaborators of Luther's in Wittenberg, while others took the Reformation back to their own countries. Bugenhagen became the great organiser of the Reformation, helping to create new church orders across northern Germany and in Scandinavia, while former students such as Peder Palladius (Denmark), Olaus Petri (Sweden), Johann Wenth (Schleswig-Holstein), Martin Krowicki (Poland), Mathias Devai (Hungary) helped shape the Reformation in their native countries. Without these personal networks, the Reformation would never have been able to spread as rapidly as it did.

For Luther, despite his focus on writing and publishing, the spoken word always remained paramount. He remained convinced throughout his life that the evangelical message was best promoted through preaching. For Luther and his colleagues, sermons were the best way to communicate and to convert people to the 'truth' – they were convinced that hearing would lead to believing.

Luther, however, became Europe's leading author overnight in the autumn of 1517 – a kind of early modern 'media-star' (Rublack, 2005, p. 45). It has been estimated that 3.1 million copies of his works were sold between 1517 and 1546, excluding his Bible translations. A fifth of the 7,500 popular broadsheets published between 1520 and 1526 are attributed to Luther and many more carried a message that supported his views. Even if we bear in mind that only a minority of early modern people could read (it has been estimated that about a third of the male population in urban areas could read, while literacy was considerably lower in the countryside where the overwhelming majority of the population lived), these are impressive numbers which must have made a considerable impact. Most of these editions of Luther's works – a total of 1,057 editions – were printed in Wittenberg between 1516 and 1546.

From the outset, Luther was also aware of the significance of the visual arts for getting his message across to the widest possible audience, especially by using its cheapest and most conveniently mass-produced form, the woodcut. In this he was assisted by Lucas Cranach the Elder, who not only designed the artwork, but from 1519 also produced much of this propaganda in his workshop in Wittenberg. Furthermore, Cranach operated not only as Luther's main illustrator, but also as his most important printer and publisher during the crucial years from 1520 to 1525, when a virtual publication explosion took place. Luther, Melanchthon and Cranach worked closely together and formed a public relations team that proved incredibly adept in taking up subjects which had caught the public imagination.

So, Luther's success in spreading the evangelical message depended to a considerable extent on the support he could rely on not only from the elector of Saxony, but from a very able team of associates and supporters who all made important contributions to the successful evangelical propaganda effort of the 1520s. Without the input of Melanchthon, Cranach, Bugenhagen and Spalatin, and the network of collaborators and students who were able to spread the evangelical message further, the speed and success of the Reformation would have been unimaginable.

WOMEN AND THE REFORMATION

As you have seen, the evangelical reformers denied that the clergy held a privileged position within the church. Their doctrine of the priesthood of all believers made any distinction between laity and clergy obsolete. They also rejected the Catholic Church's glorification of celibacy, virginity and sexual abstinence as particularly valuable Christian assets that enhanced one's chances of salvation. The reformers all encouraged the dissolution of monasteries and nunneries as unnecessary human inventions. Instead, Luther and the evangelical reformers all emphasised the importance of marriage, and virtually all of them married during the 1520s. Thus the reformers tried to give leadership to their communities and congregations in domestic as well as spiritual matters. Many of them, like Luther, married former nuns. Their wives often came to serve as models to be emulated by other evangelical women. The Reformation served to enhance the value and prestige of marriage, while countering the anti-marriage and misogynist sentiments which, according to some historians, had been prominent in the later Middle Ages. Feminist historians such as Lyndal Roper have, however, argued that the Reformation, rather than benefiting women by enhancing the value of marriage, locked them into unwanted marriages, preventing them from having an independent existence in nunneries while simultaneously destroying an important part of medieval piety that had been shaped by women (e.g. Roper, 1989). They have argued that the reformers' rejection of celibacy had the greatest impact on female orders and communities, and pointed to the often determined resistance to dissolution and conversion of their communities shown by many female orders and convents, especially within the Holy Roman Empire.

Some Reformation historians, such as Steven Ozment, have taken issue with this interpretation:

> The reformers had no concept whatsoever of the cloister as a special 'woman's place,' where women might gain a degree of freedom and authority denied them in the secular world, while at the same time escaping the drudgery of marriage, the domination of husbands, and the debilities of serial pregnancies and motherhood. Had such an argument been made to them, the reformers would surely have condemned it as an unnatural and unchristian attempt on the part of women to escape their God-given responsibilities in life. They would also surely have marveled at the spectacle of modern feminist scholars identifying with the cloistered women of the Middle Ages, to the sixteenth-century Protestant mind, their age's most sexually repressed group.
>
> (Ozment, 1993, p. 154).

EXERCISE

Now read Chapter 6 of the set book by Wallace, pp. 202–16. Note the answer Wallace provides for his question about whether or not women had a reformation.

Spend about 20 minutes on this exercise.

Even if it remains debatable how women were affected by the Reformation, there is general agreement that the Reformation provided some women with new opportunities, especially during the dramatic and revolutionary years of the early 1520s. One such woman was Argula von Grumbach, an impoverished noblewomen who had lost her parents to plague at an early age. Unlike some other well-educated noblewomen, Argula had no Latin. She had been given a copy of the German Coburg Bible (1483) by her father at an early age and told to read it thoroughly, but had been discouraged by her Franciscan teachers, who had warned her that it might easily lead her to heresy. She appears to have taken considerable interest in theology and religious issues early on and later corresponded with several of the evangelical reformers, including Luther and Spalatin in Wittenberg and Andreas Osiander in Nuremberg. From 1523 to 1524, Argula von Grumbach published no less than eight pamphlets. She entered the Reformation debate by intervening in the Arsacius Seehofer affair at Ingolstadt by publishing her first pamphlet entitled: 'A Christian noblewoman from Bavaria's missive to the faculty in Ingolstadt, in which she uses holy scripture to defend an evangelical young man' (1523) (see Figure 6.10). It was probably through her brother, then a student at the University of Ingolstadt, that Argula had come to hear of Seehofer, a student and instructor, who had been charged with Lutheran heresy by the university authorities after a search of his quarters had turned up a number of Lutheran pamphlets and letters expressing evangelical ideas. Seehofer was then forced to recant his evangelical doctrines as the work of the Devil and heresy.

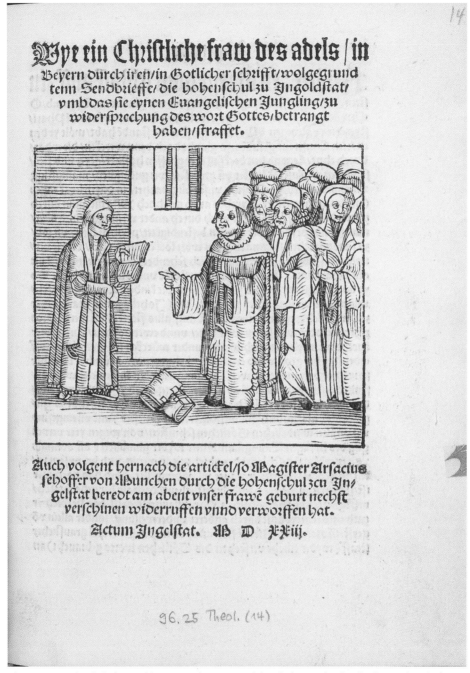

Figure 6.10   'A Christian noblewoman from Bavaria's missive to the faculty in Ingolstadt, in which she uses holy scripture to defend an evangelical young man', 1523, frontispiece. Photo: Herzog August Bibliothek, Wolfenbüttel, Germany, 96.25 Theol. (14)

EXERCISE

Now read Anthology Document 2.5, 'Argula von Grumbach, "A Christian noblewoman's missive", 1523', and answer the following questions:

1   Why are the writings of Luther and Melanchthon true, according to Argula von Grumbach?

2   Why does Argula von Grumbach consider the pope in league with the Devil in his treatment of women?

Spend about 15 minutes on this exercise.

SPECIMEN ANSWER

1   Because they are in accordance with the Gospel.

2   By insisting on celibacy and preventing the clergy from marrying, the pope has turned women into concubines.

Being well read in the Bible, Argula von Grumbach was, of course, familiar with the views of Paul that women should neither teach nor preach in the Christian community. She justified her intervention, however, by claiming that in extreme situations, such as the present, such considerations should be waived:

> I am not unfamiliar with Paul's words that women should be silent in church but when I see that no man will or can speak, I am driven by the word of God when he said, he who confesses me on earth, him will I confess and he who denies me, him will I deny.
>
> (Wiesner, 1993, pp. 187–8)

As much as being a defence of Seehofer, Argula von Grumbach's pamphlet was a defence of the evangelical cause.

REFERENCES

Beutel, A. (2003) 'Luther's life' in McKim, D.K. (ed.) *The Cambridge Companion to Martin Luther*, Cambridge, Cambridge University Press.

Collinson, P. (2003) *The Reformation*, London, Weidenfeld & Nicolson.

Cunningham, A. and Grell, O.P. (2000) *The Four Horsemen of the Apocalypse. Religion, War, Famine and Death in Reformation Europe*, Cambridge, Cambridge University Press.

MacCulloch, D. (2003) *Reformation. Europe's House Divided*, London, Penguin.

Ozment, S. (1993) *Protestants. The Birth of a Revolution*, London, Fontana.

Roper, L. (1989) *The Holy Household: Women and Morals in Reformation Augsburg*, Oxford, Clarendon Press.

Rublack, U. (2005) *Reformation Europe*, Cambridge, Cambridge University Press.

Scribner, R.W. (1994) *For the Sake of Simple Folk. Popular Propaganda for the German Reformation*, Oxford, Oxford University Press.

Wiesner, M.E. (1993) *Women and Gender in Early Modern Europe*, Cambridge, Cambridge University Press.

Ole Peter Grell, Anne Laurence and Donna Loftus

INTRODUCTION

In this unit we shall look at reform in two different locations in a predominantly urban context. You might think that we can scarcely call the Low Countries a city environment, but the territory that we now know as Belgium and the Netherlands (Holland is merely one of the provinces of the Netherlands) was by far the most urbanised part of Europe, and around half the population lived in towns. Equally, Geneva was not just a city, it was an autonomous city-state that keenly guarded its independence.

Reform in each of these locations was not just about changes in religious doctrine and practice, it was about the identity of the citizens and their sense of nationhood or citizenship. In Geneva you will look at the attempt to create a godly commonwealth, while in the Netherlands you will consider whether the Dutch revolt was primarily about religious freedom or about liberation from the Habsburg yoke. This unit is not just about beliefs and ideologies, it is also about state formation and, because of the desire of these places for political and economic autonomy, about producers and consumers. The aim of this unit is to allow you to see how religious reform played out in different ways in different locations, in both cases producing significant variations from Luther's reformation and the progress of reform in Germany.

You will again be reading a good deal from the set book for this module, Peter Wallace, *The Long European Reformation*, and the unit will offer a commentary on his views, not always in agreement with him.

EXERCISE

Read the section 'The Reformation negotiated: urban reformations' in the set book by Wallace, pp. 89–93. What does Wallace suggest were the most important elements of reform in the towns?

Spend about 15 minutes on this exercise.

SPECIMEN ANSWER

Wallace emphasises the large, urban audiences available to listen to the sermons of the evangelical preachers and the considerable market in urban areas for the rapidly expanding number of evangelical pamphlets. The government of towns by elected assemblies, rather than by landowners, and the direct engagement of citizens, both men and women, with the urban authorities was important. Wallace writes, too, of the systematic eradication of Catholic institutions after 1525.

Wallace refers to the splits developing within the evangelical movement, with the followers of Martin Bucer (Figure 7.1) and Heinrich Zwingli diverging from Luther's vision. He also raises the question of how many people really did subscribe to the new practices and beliefs.

Figure 7.1   Artist unknown, *Martin Bucer*, 1586, woodcut. Germanisches Nationalmuseum, Nuremberg, Inv.-Nr. Mp. 3061. Photo: Germanisches Nationalmuseum

You have seen in Unit 6 that religious reform in Germany was centred on towns such as Wittenberg, not least because of the high levels of urban literacy. Towns were also the places where the Catholic priests, monks and nuns were most visible. In the larger cities they were present in their hundreds, easily identifiable by their clothing. They and their institutions, such as monasteries and convents, were prominent in the early modern urban landscape. The privileges they enjoyed, such as exemption from taxation and from civic duties, often made them unpopular even though they were engaged in much charitable activity, such as running hospitals and schools.

Towns also had their own local government. What is of particular significance for this unit is the close involvement of the municipal authorities with the reforming clergy and congregations: secular and religious government were no longer separate entities.

THE REFORMATION IN GENEVA

In the early sixteenth century, Geneva was a regionally important, but relatively modest, trading city of around 10,000 people. It had recently secured its independence from its Catholic bishop and the duke of Savoy, having been assisted in its struggle for independence by the neighbouring Swiss city-state of Berne, with whom the civic leaders of Geneva established an alliance. The city was ruled by a number of interlocking councils, whose members were selected from the minority of men who were full citizens. By the mid sixteenth century it was regarded as the second seat of the Reformation, and its population had swelled to 17,000, primarily through an influx of Protestant refugees from France. Wallace, pp. 103–6, gives a general outline of reform in Geneva – you may want to read this before proceeding.

John Calvin (1509–1564) (see Figure 7.2) fled France for Basle and was on his way to Strasburg in July 1536 when he stopped over in Geneva. Here he met the reformer William Farel (1489–1565), who convinced him to stay and join him in his attempt to reform the city. However, by 1538, Calvin and Farel had fallen out with the Genevan magistracy. The clash occurred over the question of ecclesiastical discipline. Calvin had composed a confession of faith that he wanted all the citizens of Geneva to accept. By 1538, Calvin and Farel had decided that those citizens who were opposed to the confession should be excluded from Communion. The magistracy intervened, stating that no one should be excluded from Communion for that reason, thereby not only emphasising its willingness to intervene in religious affairs, but laying claim to supremacy over the clergy in ecclesiastical matters. Further intervention by the city council in church affairs brought matters to a head when the Protestant ministers abstained from celebrating Communion on Easter Day 1538. In response, the magistracy immediately dismissed Farel and Calvin and ordered them to leave Geneva within three days.

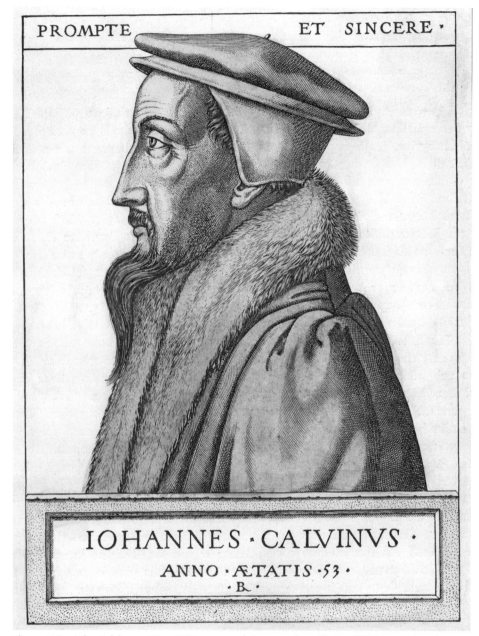

Figure 7.2   *John Calvin age 53, c.*1562, copperplate engraving. Photo: AKG-Images, London

Having been expelled from Geneva, Calvin set out for his first intended destination, Strasburg (see Figure 7.3), where on the invitation of the city's leading reformer, Martin Bucer (1491–1551), he took over responsibility for the refugee French church in the city. During his sojourn in Strasburg, Calvin's convictions about the nature of church government were strongly influenced by Bucer.

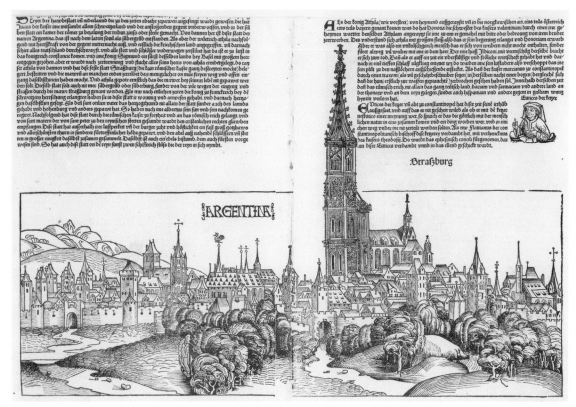

Figure 7.3   Strasburg (1493), from Hartmann Schedel's *Weltchronik*. Germanisches Nationalmuseum, Nuremberg, Inv.-Nr. S.P. 3221 Kaps 1131. Photo: Germanisches Nationalmuseum

Bucer might also have been the inspiration for Calvin's adoption of the doctrine of predestination, according to which God had decided who was to be saved and who was to be eternally damned.

EXERCISE

Read Anthology Document 2.10, which is an extract from Calvin's *Institutes of the Christian Religion*, Book 3, Chapter 21, and answer the following questions:

1   How, according to Calvin, did God decide who are foreordained to be saved and who to be damned?

2   Can we have any idea of who will be saved and who will be damned?

Spend about 25 minutes on this exercise.

SPECIMEN ANSWER

1   God made His eternal decision by extending His mercy freely and irrespective of human worth to those whom He wanted to be saved, while those facing damnation had been condemned by a 'just ... but ... incomprehensible judgment'.

2   Yes. Those who are to be saved, the elect, are visible through their 'calling and justification', while those who will be damned are excluded from 'knowledge of his name' or 'sanctification of his Spirit'. In other words, this latter group do not belong to the true, visible church where the elect, on the other hand, are highly visible, serving the godly community as deacons, elders and ministers.

Predestination was *not* exclusive to Calvin. However, the fact that Calvin was forced by his opponents to explore and defend this doctrine, at the same time as Philip Melanchthon was softening the Lutheran approach to these issues, has identified this doctrine with Calvin; in reality it was Calvin's successor in Geneva, Theodore Beza (1519–1605), who raised the doctrine of predestination to its pre-eminence within Calvinism.

The clash between Farel and Calvin and the city's governors was less about religion than about authority. Genevan civic leaders had no doubt that they had the right to change the religious practices of the city without needing the approval of the Protestant ministers. The majority of the council (the Articulants) believed that the confession of Farel and Calvin jeopardised the city's power over its clergy, though by 1540 the leaders of the minority faction that supported Calvin and Farel had won control.

The consolidation of the Reformation in Geneva

It was with hesitation that Calvin accepted the recall from the new civic leaders in Geneva in October 1541. Although Calvin's return is regarded as signalling the change in Geneva's ecclesiastical policy, the faction that supported him had already been back in power for more than a year before they recalled Calvin, and they did not repeal any of the ecclesiastical changes to which Calvin had objected before his return. Everything indicates that the ecclesiastical and religious aspects of the 1538–41 crisis were of secondary importance. The recall of Calvin came only after the two ministers who had been hired to replace him and Farel in 1538 abandoned their positions and left the city.

EXERCISE	Turn to Anthology Document 2.11, 'Establishment of Calvinism in Switzerland', and read Calvin's letter (a) to Oswald Myconius (1488–1552), the leading Protestant minister in Basle, dated 14 March 1542. Then answer the following questions:

1   Who does Calvin identify as his main opponents in Geneva in 1542?

2   How does he propose to deal with them?

Spend about 25 minutes on this exercise.

SPECIMEN ANSWER	1 His ministerial colleagues and some members of the magistracy.
	2 With forbearance and tolerance.

DISCUSSION	1 Calvin points his finger at his colleagues (i.e. the ministers who had remained in Geneva after he and Farel had been expelled). They showed him little respect, were unlearned and demonstrated little or no commitment to the Reformation. They, however, were not the only ones hampering Calvin's work. Some members of the magistracy ('many in their assembly') were far from friendly, while others were openly hostile to him. Calvin provided an example of how his colleagues within the ministry undermined him. After publicly having supported the introduction of 'ecclesiastical censure', as suggested by Calvin, some of his colleagues discreetly approached members of the civic leadership, pointing out

to them the dangers of surrendering the right of excommunication to the pastors and the consistories, which might lead to disorder and revolt.

2   Calvin claimed that he showed his colleagues forbearance and humoured them. He had no intention of disturbing the 'peace of the church', as he put it. Instead of having them ousted on his return, he had been determined to show himself as a moderate who did his utmost to prevent discord among the clergy, which would prove particularly damaging if it became known among 'the common people'. Referring to the activities of Farel's pupil Pierre Viret (1511–1571) in Geneva as being particularly 'pleasant and humane', Calvin emphasised his own efforts to generate peace and cordiality, claiming that as a result some of those who had previously been his enemies were now his friends. Calvin, in his own opinion, had clearly surprised many of his antagonists by his unexpected tolerance and spirit of compromise.

On his return, Calvin had set about drafting a church order for Geneva, *The Ecclesiastical Ordinances of 1541*, which drew heavily on his Strasburg experience and on inspiration from Bucer. The ordinances introduced the four ministries of the church (pastors, teachers, elders and deacons) and gave detailed instructions for their appointment. New ministers were to be examined and nominated by the sitting ministers who constituted the Company of Pastors; successful candidates would then be reviewed by the magistracy and, if accepted, presented to the congregation. Elders were to be:

> men of virtuous lives, honest, without reproach and beyond all suspicion, above all God-fearing and of good spiritual prudence. And, they should be elected in such a manner that there will be some of them in each quarter of the city, so that their eyes will be everywhere.
> (Lindberg, 2000, p. 171)

Calvin and his supporters also wanted to create a godly society in which the invisible church of the elect became visible. This moral reform had the support of a substantial part of the population and was enforced by orders issued by the city council, often on the encouragement of Calvin and the Company of Pastors. In 1544, the magistracy issued an order, after having received a complaint from Calvin, forbidding the singing of immoral songs and loitering in the streets during the Sunday sermon (Benedict, 2002, p. 98).

Calvin soon realised that, if he was to have any success in reforming the Genevan church along the lines set out in *The Ecclesiastical Ordinances of 1541*, he required loyal ministerial colleagues and elders who shared his vision for a godly society; the Company of Pastors needed to be expanded and cleansed of disloyal elements. However, Calvin was faced with a group of ministers whose understanding of the relationship between church and state was different from his. Despite his claim in his letter to Myconius that he tolerated these colleagues for the sake of peace in the community, Calvin was clearly determined to have them removed. By 1546, the Company of Pastors had lost nearly all the ministers with whom Calvin disagreed or who fell short of his expectations, and he had assembled a religiously unified group of trusted and well-educated colleagues of high social standing around him.

The calibre of this new cohort of ministers is evident from the religious works they published. At the same time, these ministers did not rely exclusively on the salaries they received from the magistracy. However, pastors continued to be exclusively recruited from French refugees and Jacques Bernard remained the only exception to this rule.

The Company of Pastors, however, constituted only one part of the consistory, which ruled the church. Its twelve lay members, the elders, were elected from the city councils, and for Calvin it was of the utmost importance for stability and continuity that they were committed Christians who were prepared to serve the church for a number of years. By 1546, Calvin had achieved considerable success when a core of seven elders was elected to serve the church for the next seven years, though only one or two of these belonged to leading Genevan families, and none held prominent positions within the magistracy. So, by 1546–47, Calvin had managed to create a socially and educationally unified body of pastors in Geneva, and he had succeeded in establishing a committed group of elders who were prepared to assist their clerical colleagues in the consistory. Elderships appear to have held little political prestige in Geneva in the 1540s: by 1555 that was to change, when five of the elders would obtain powerful positions within the city's magistracy as a consequence of Calvin's victory over his opponents.

The political unity that had led to Calvin's recall in 1541 was, however, disappearing by 1546, and a new period of political division, which would culminate in the crisis of 1555, was about to begin. By 1546, a clash between the magistracy of Geneva, whose personnel had changed considerably since Calvin's return, and an increasingly self-confident Company of Pastors, backed by the consistory, seemed difficult to avoid.

Opposition to Calvin's vision of a godly society

The first major confrontation arose from the festivities surrounding the wedding of the daughter of an influential Genevan, Antoine Lect, at which some of the guests had engaged in dancing, despite it having recently been made unlawful in Geneva. Twenty-six people were arrested, including members of the influential Favre and Bonna families, among them several members of the magistracy.

EXERCISE

Turn to Anthology Document 2.11, 'Establishment of Calvinism in Switzerland', and read the extract from Calvin's letter (b) to William Farel, dated April 1546.

1   What does this letter tell us about Calvin's willingness to punish immoral behaviour in Geneva?

2   What do you think the legacy of this incident would have been among those arrested?

Spend about 20 minutes on this exercise.

1   Calvin wanted all transgressors punished, irrespective of their social status.

2   A legacy of resentment towards Calvin and the Company of Pastors.

1   Calvin was evidently prepared to pursue any person suspected of immoral behaviour, irrespective of his/her social position. He was further incensed by the willingness of the majority of those accused to add to their sins by lying. Calvin was evidently pleased with the public effect of his actions, which he claimed had made people realise that any moral transgression would be punished immediately without favouritism.

2   The humiliation of some of the most prominent Genevans by Calvin and the consistory cannot but have generated anger and hatred, and left a legacy of bitterness and animosity towards Calvin and his fellow pastors. Even someone like the presiding syndic, Amblard Corne, who had admitted to dancing and blamed himself and others for having undertaken the act, was deposed until he had 'given proof of repentance'. Ami Perrin, another magistrate who had admitted to dancing, was not able to escape punishment either, despite conveniently undertaking a trip to Lyon immediately afterwards; he was imprisoned on his return. Calvin appeared unconcerned that both Perrin and his wife were deeply angered about the episode and their imprisonment.

Calvin demonstrated his determination to pursue the case and get to the bottom of it. He used the pulpit to launch a major attack on the lack of morality in Geneva, accusing the dancers of being 'ruffians'. The sermon caused a storm of protest and the service was disrupted. A member of the city magistracy was so angry that he stood up and took issue with Calvin. Calvin and the Company of Pastors, however, refused to budge and, after a fortnight's imprisonment, the resolve of those arrested was broken and they repented.

The year 1546 witnessed a growing number of clashes between leading Genevans and the immigrant French ministers of the Company of Pastors. Many prominent citizens had begun to see Calvin and his fellow Frenchmen in the Company of Pastors as power-hungry and arrogant, while Calvin interpreted the escalating conflicts as the consequence of some Genevans' unwillingness to live truly godly lives and submit themselves to Christian discipline. This confrontation ended in late July 1546 with the outbreak of the Schmalkaldic War in Germany and an upsurge in religious persecution in France.

The priorities of the civic leaders changed overnight. Faced with the possibility that the city might be drawn into the religious conflict in Germany, the magistracy made considerable efforts to quell all internal turmoil. In March 1547, Calvin and members of the Favre family and their supporters were called before one of the city councils and ordered to be reconciled. The number of French refugees arriving in Geneva also began to worry the magistracy.

By mid-1549, the threat of an attack by Catholic imperial forces was receding but major public disturbances and riots erupted in the city, connected with attacks on the rapidly growing number of French refugees. Furthermore, the number of clashes between citizens and the Company of Pastors began to increase, especially in the area of sexual immorality. Citizens believed that arrogant French ministers were attempting to govern their private lives, while Calvin and his co-pastors saw it as proof that many Genevans were disinclined to reform their morals.

The most frequent clashes, however, occurred over baptismal names. Naming a child not only defined him or her as a human being, it also placed the child within the family and within the community. Conflicts arose from ministers' attempt to ban traditional names, which they considered to originate in Catholic superstition. They wanted to eliminate all names that weren't biblical, even those of the local saints Claude and Martin.

The crisis over names began in August 1546, when a barber presented his son for baptism. The minister was informed that the child's name was to be Claude, which he ignored in favour of baptising the boy Abraham. The father angrily grabbed his son and declared that no true baptism had taken place, and that he would let his son remain unbaptised until he turned fifteen, so he could choose his own name. The congregation objected to what they considered the minister's scandalous action. The disturbance that followed led to an enquiry during which the ministers managed to convince the magistracy to ban the use of the name Claude because of its association with a nearby shrine. But further clashes followed. By the spring of 1547, the magistracy withdrew its backing for the ministers in what had become a serious confrontation with the city's native population.

The altercation also generated a strong xenophobic reaction against the predominantly French Company of Pastors. Ministers wanted to use civil sanctions and excommunication against citizens who opposed their policy on baptismal names; the magistracy warned the ministers that they had exceeded their authority in the confrontation over baptismal names. This intervention, however, appears to have had little or no effect, and the dispute drew in more and more influential Genevans, even members of the magistracy, during the following year.

The creation of a godly society

The growing xenophobia in Geneva had much to do with the large waves of French refugees who arrived during these years. More than 5,000 heads of households from France applied for residence permits in the city between 1549 and 1560. Considering the city's size, this would have amounted to more than a 50 per cent increase in the city's population.

By the early 1550s, factional conflict between those who opposed the growing influence of the French ministers and the expanding community of French refugees in the city had coalesced around Ami Perrin. These 'Perrinists', or libertines, suggested at the 1551 municipal elections that limitations be put on rights accorded to refugees granted the status of citizens. They were unsuccessful on this occasion, but at the following year's election they were able to increase their influence within the magistracy, although their victory did not manage to curtail the influence of the French refugees in the city.

Factional disputes and clashes between citizens and pastors continued. The ministers, and Calvin in particular, drove home their views from the pulpits. They claimed that the city's immorality was the cause of all the troubles; only a godly magistracy could avert the punishing hand of God. Calvin himself on the eve of the 1555 elections denounced the city's leaders as morally suspect, claiming that only he and his supporters could restore godliness and avert God's wrath.

This message clearly had an impact, and the elections of 1555 showed a swing towards Calvin and his supporters, who used their slim victory to good effect, increasing the number of their supporters in the Genevan electorate at a stroke by awarding bourgeois status to a group of French, pro-Calvin refugees. Perrinist objectors took to the streets of Geneva; on the evening of 16 May, their frustration and anger spilt over into riot.

EXERCISE

Turn to Anthology Document 2.11, 'Establishment of Calvinism in Switzerland', and read Calvin's letter (c) to Heinrich Bullinger in Zurich, dated 15 June 1555.

1   How does Calvin describe his Perrinist opponents?

2   How serious was the riot on 16 May 1555, according to Calvin?

Spend about 25 minutes on this exercise.

SPECIMEN ANSWER

1   Calvin first describes the leaders, Ami Perrin and Pierre Vandel, as two 'unprincipled' and impudent members of the Small Council. According to Calvin, Perrin had been able to recruit a group of reckless and dissolute people by promising them that they could act with impunity because, whatever they did, Perrin would personally protect them. By applying pressure and threats, the Perrinists had been able to build up support within the Small Council. Their hold on the Council had been reinforced by their many relations among the councillors. The Perrinists were, in other words, deeply corrupt and they had corrupted all judicial proceedings in Geneva. They had also successfully packed the Council of Two Hundred with their supporters, whom Calvin described as the dregs of society.

2   The riot was a serious affair according to Calvin (despite the fact that Geneva had experienced plenty of riots in the decade leading up to 1555). The riot began in the middle of the night and nearly caused the city government and state to collapse. However, Calvin's description of how a dinner given by Perrin and Vandel for their supporters led some of the guests into trouble with the city guards cannot help but give the impression that the event was more likely to have been rooted in a drunken brawl rather than in well-planned and premeditated action. Even in Calvin's version one gets the distinct impression that the riot only turned into a 'serious event' after an inquiry was set up and those accused removed from their positions within the magistracy and judiciary – actions that caused a number of the leaders of the Perrinist faction, including Ami Perrin, to flee Geneva.

There is no evidence to support Calvin's contention that the riot was an attempt to overthrow the government of Geneva. There were a few arrests, but initially no action was taken against the Perrinist leaders. It was not until 25 May, nine days after the riot, that the dominant Calvinist faction within the city government realised the potential the riot had offered them for destroying their opponents. During the summer, twenty of the rioters were sentenced to death, most of whom had already fled the city for Berne, but at least six were executed. More were fined or disenfranchised. Calvin and his supporters saw themselves as God's instruments and the Perrinists as sinful enemies of God, providing religious justification for their action.

The execution and forced exile of so many prominent Genevans caused much alarm in other Protestant cities in Switzerland. Bullinger in Zurich, the recipient of Calvin's explanatory letter about the riot, received many letters objecting to the actions taken by the Calvinist party in Geneva. When, in September 1555, he responded to Calvin's letter of 15 June, he emphasised the anger that the treatment of the Perrinists had given rise to. Unpopularity, however, was a price the Calvinist party in Geneva was prepared to pay if the prize was a consolidation and expansion of their power.

As the case of Geneva shows, the Reformation was about much more than religious beliefs: questions of religion, authority and legitimate governance were closely intertwined.

REFORM IN THE NETHERLANDS

Evangelical ideas reached the Netherlands in the early 1520s. Here, as elsewhere, Luther provided the inspiration for the early reform movement, though political conditions there were, however, far from favourable to the adoption of his ideas. In contrast to the Holy Roman Empire, where, as you have seen, the power of Emperor Charles V was severely restricted by the territorial princes, many of whom were willing to protect the evangelical movement, Charles V reigned in the Netherlands without such limitations. The Netherlands were part of his inherited domain, some of which he had received in his capacity as duke of Burgundy. The importance of this wealthy urbanised region for Charles V's power is difficult to overestimate (not unlike the position of Burgundy in the previous century, as you saw in Block 1). The seventeen densely populated provinces of the Netherlands together constituted one of the most dynamic economies of early modern Europe. In the southern provinces, Antwerp was developing into the leading mercantile metropolis of Europe (see Figure 7.4). The French printer Christopher Plantin settled in Antwerp in 1549, explaining that:

> No other town in the world could offer me more facilities for carrying on the trade I intended to begin. Antwerp can be easily reached; various nations meet in its market-place; there too can be found the raw materials indispensable for the practice of ones trade; craftsmen for all trades can easily be found and instructed in a short time.
>
> (Parker, 1979, p. 26)

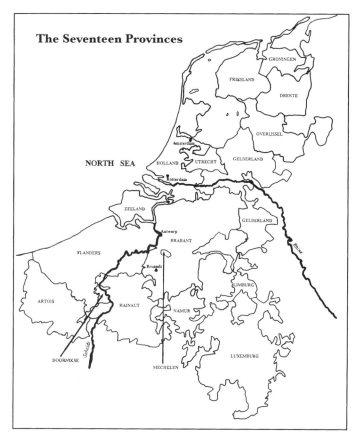

Figure 7.4 The seventeen provinces of the Netherlands (1550), from James Tanis and Daniel Horst (1993) *Images of Discord: A Graphic Interpretation of the Opening Decades of the Eighty Years' War*, Michigan: Wm. B. Eerdmans Publishing Co., p. x

EXERCISE

Read the section 'Revolt and Reformation in the Netherlands' in the set book by Wallace, pp. 139–44. What were the most important aspects of the government and state of the Netherlands on the eve of the Reformation?

Spend about 20 minutes on this exercise.

SPECIMEN ANSWER

Wallace emphasises mainly three aspects:

1 the relative weakness of the government of Charles V in Brussels

2 the regional character of the Netherlands in terms of both language and culture

3 the considerable political independence of many of the provinces that made up the Netherlands.

The seventeen provinces of the Netherlands were only gradually emerging as a state by the early sixteenth century, the territory's political development often hampered by regionalism and the defence of individual provinces' privileges by the provincial states. These bodies were powerful institutions that could levy and collect taxes and raise troops. Every three years these assemblies met together as the states general to discuss tax demands, but had no power independent of the provinces to put their decisions into effect. Furthermore, there were considerable cultural and legal differences between many of the northern and southern provinces: the language of the north was Dutch while that of the south was predominantly French/Walloon.

The influence of Calvinism

Calvinism, which proved so important for the spread of the Reformed faith in France, was slow in making an impact in the Netherlands, even in the French/Walloon-speaking areas. Evangelical services remained clandestine and many Protestants continued to attend Mass because of the considerable personal risks associated with openly becoming a Protestant. This attitude of compromise hampered the growth of Protestantism.

The first Reformed church in the Netherlands was established at Antwerp in 1555, in the same year that the Huguenots established their first church in Paris. But the spread of reform was very different; in 1561, the Huguenot leader Gaspar de Coligny claimed there were more than 1,750 Reformed congregations in France while in the Netherlands there were only twelve, of which two alone were in the southern French/Walloon-speaking areas.

However, this situation was transformed by the arrival in the southern Netherlands of large numbers of French Reformed refugees (Huguenots) fleeing persecution and the first French War of Religion (1562–70). Huguenot refugees not only boosted the number of Reformed congregations, but also guaranteed that the influence of Calvin and Geneva rapidly replaced the earlier close contacts between Flanders and German centres of the Reformation. During the 1560s, perhaps as many as 300 new 'churches under the cross' (i.e. clandestine congregations) came into existence in the southern Netherlands. By 1562, the number of Reformed communities in Antwerp justified the establishment of a formal organisation, modelled on the four-tier structure of the Genevan and the Huguenot churches in France of the consistory (the individual congregation), the classis (regional groups of congregations) and the provincial synod (all congregations in the province), and finally the national synod.

The Reformed communities in the northern Dutch-speaking areas of the Netherlands drew on a number of reformers for inspiration, The theological writings of Johannes a Lasco (1499–1560) and Martin Micronius (1523–1559) were initially of far greater significance to these early Dutch Reformed communities than Calvin's. Only a minority of the ministers who served the 'churches under the cross' in the Netherlands had attended the Academy of Geneva, which had been set up in 1559 to train Calvinist ministers. The majority were educated at the University of Heidelberg and often trained in the Dutch and Walloon churches in Emden and London who also supplied funds.

The crisis of 1566

In 1556, Philip II (*1556–1598) succeeded his father, Charles V, as king of Spain and of the Habsburg Netherlands. He was brought up exclusively in Spain, but spent four years of his young adulthood in the Netherlands, from 1555 to 1559. Despite that, Philip, a conservative Catholic, remained a stranger to the cultural and political traditions of the Netherlands.

The uprising in 1566 was brought about by a mixture of political, economic and religious grievances against the king and his representative in the Netherlands, his half-sister Margaret (1522–1586), duchess of Parma and governess-general of the Netherlands from 1559 to 1567. Taxation had soared in the Netherlands as a consequence of Philip II's victorious but costly war with France from 1557 to 1559. To the disquiet over tax increases were added the complaints of the local nobility about the policies introduced by Margaret's chief advisor, Cardinal Granvelle (1517–1586). Granvelle wanted to reorganise the Catholic bishoprics in the Netherlands in order to improve their financial, administrative and religious performance and to eliminate heresy. So forceful was the opposition of local magnates, who saw this as a process of centralisation that would reduce their influence, that Philip II was obliged to dismiss Granvelle in December 1564. Local magnates, such as William of Orange (1533–1584) and the counts of Egmond (1522–1568) and Horn (1524–1568), clearly hoped that this was to be a first step towards the cessation of religious persecution. They interpreted Philip II's year-long silence as a sign that the king was prepared to change his policies.

Philip, however, chose to continue his policy of religious persecution through his edicts and the Inquisition. Things came to a head when Margaret attempted to enforce his heresy laws in a proclamation of 20 December 1565. This prompted a group of local noblemen, led by William of Orange, the count of Culemborg and the baron of Brederode to draw up the Petition of Compromise, also known as the Request. It was presented to the governess-general on 5 April 1566 by William of Orange accompanied by 200 armed confederates, nicknamed Les Gueux (the Beggars) because they all wore grey. The name quickly became associated with opposition to Spanish rule and was later, in 1572, transferred to the famous irregular naval force which took the lead in the fight with the Spaniards: the Sea Beggars.

EXERCISE

Read Anthology Document 2.21, 'Petition of Compromise, 5 April 1566'. What is the petition concerned with and what is it asking Philip II to do?

Spend about 25 minutes on this exercise.

SPECIMEN ANSWER

It is concerned with religious issues and seeks to have all religious persecution suspended.

DISCUSSION

The emphasis was on religion. The petitioners, however, did not refer to the subject directly nor to the Protestants or those of the Reformed faith especially. By rigorously seeking to execute his edicts and by using the Inquisition, the king might well cause 'open revolt and a universal rebellion' which could destroy the fabric of society in all the provinces of the Netherlands.

In order to prevent these dangers, the petitioners requested Philip II not only not to enforce the edicts, but to repeal them and to suspend the Inquisition. In this they were supported by Margaret of Parma, as long as they promised not to undertake any religious changes in the different provinces, but would uphold 'the ancient religion' (i.e. the Catholic Church).

The Petition of Compromise was a finely tuned instrument which emphasised the loyalty of the Beggars to the crown and the Catholic Church. It focused exclusively on the Inquisition and the religious edicts that the petitioners wanted removed because they represented a danger to the government. The petitioners emphasised their loyalty to king and church and only advocated the removal of an institution, the Inquisition, that was so hated that it could lead to rebellion. Margaret of Parma had no option but to let the petitioners have their way. She suspended the heresy laws while a delegation from the states general travelled to Spain to negotiate with Philip II. The Petition of Compromise thus had the desired result: persecution was halted, even if public meetings of what the Spanish government labelled heretics (i.e. Protestants) were still prohibited.

The political initiative now lay with the local nobility who supported William of Orange and the baron of Brederode, the so-called confederates. Brederode was particularly active in drumming up support for the petition by taking it from town to town and encouraging civic leaders and other members of the nobility to sign it. It proved especially successful in the provinces of Flanders, Brabant and Holland, while popular demonstrations in support of the Beggars took place in Haarlem and Amsterdam.

Protestant exiles, who had emigrated in the 1540s to avoid religious persecution, now began to return, and hedge-preaching (open-air services) by Calvinist preachers began to take place, first in the southern provinces, especially Flanders. By June, they had become mass gatherings, often of hundreds and sometimes of thousands of people. Outside Antwerp, 30,000 people are supposed to have attended one of these services, which were generally held outside the jurisdiction of urban authorities, often on land belonging to noblemen of the Reformed faith. What the Reformed were to name the 'Wonderyear' had begun.

EXERCISE

Read Anthology Document 2.22, 'Two accounts of hedge-preaching in the Netherlands, 1566' (these took place in Flanders in June 1566 and in Ghent in July 1566), and then answer the following questions:

1   What were the attitudes of the authors of these accounts to hedge-preaching?

2   How similar are the events reported in the two accounts?

3   On the basis of these accounts, how successful do you think the hedge-preaching was in converting people to the Reformed faith?

Spend about 25 minutes on this exercise.

1 The first account was written by the governor of Lille, baron de Rassenghien, acting for the government in Brussels. As such he was, of course, hostile to the phenomenon. He was worried that the hedge-preaching might lead to civil disorder and violence. He was particularly worried that those members of the nobility in the 'Low Countries' (the Netherlands) who were behind the Petition of Compromise might join hands with the hedge-preachers and their followers. The second account was written by a sceptical and worried observer, Marcus van Vaernewijk, who, unlike the writer of the first account, was present at the events he described. It is noteworthy that the social-radical aspects of the hedge-preaching are far more prominent in his account. This might, of course, be rooted in the simple fact that the two accounts describe two separate events.

2 The two reports give fairly similar descriptions of the hedge-preaching. The events took place in the countryside, but in the vicinity of towns. They were well attended, drawing thousands of people. The preachers would appear to have been escorted and protected by a type of bodyguard. The twenty 'hackbutters' (arquebussiers) mentioned by the governor of Lille, who helped the preacher disappear so rapidly that it was impossible to say where he had gone, clearly served in this capacity. So did the six people escorting the preacher into the enclosure referred to in the second report. These escorts made it difficult to identify the preacher until he began his sermon. They were, in other words, precautions that made it difficult for the authorities to arrest the preachers. There are significant differences between the two reports. The named preacher in the first account appears to have been far more moderate than the unnamed preacher in the second report. The first preacher went out of his way to discourage his audience from taking the law into their own hands and encouraged them to respect civil authority. The second account is far more detailed. Here the preacher appears to have been supported by something akin to a congregation, consisting of around ninety people, divided into three groups of thirty, each with its own leader or teacher, who had their own psalm books from which they sang. They were surrounded by large numbers of curious onlookers who had been attracted to this unusual event. The message here was far more radical, namely that people should obey the Word of God and defy human laws that were not in accordance with the Word of God.

3 Only the second report provides any information about the impact of the hedge-preaching on those who had not yet joined the Reformed communities. Clearly, van Vaernewijk's washerwoman was attracted to the message of the Reformed preachers which she, despite his warnings, found edifying. According to van Vaernewijk, most of the converts came from the 'common people' who, because of their lack of education, uncritically accepted the preacher's claim that he preached the pure Word of God, and who converted in large numbers.

Within five months, hedge-preaching had become a mass phenomenon across the whole of the Netherlands. By midsummer 1566, the confederates or Beggars had lost the political initiative to the Reformed preachers and their supporters, many of whom had returned from exile in Germany, Switzerland and England. Their preaching took place in the context of a growing economic crisis. In the power vacuum that opened up with the suspension of religious persecution and government paralysis it was always highly likely that some form of popular reaction against the Catholic Church would result. This was encouraged by a militant minority of Reformed preachers who legitimised the use of force to achieve a reformation.

On 10 August 1566, the *beeldenstorm* (iconoclasm) began in west Flanders when crowds, having attended a Reformed sermon, attacked a local convent and smashed the religious images. These Catholic images were denounced by the evangelical preachers as superstitious and unbiblical. For early Protestants, Catholic statues of saints and stained-glass images were seen as synonymous with the perceived false teachings of the church, urgently to be dismantled and reformed. Protestants saw these images as human inventions in direct opposition to the second of the Ten Commandments. Veneration of saints (and, by extension, their images) contradicted reformers' emphasis on faith and grace alone as the way to salvation. Images came to be a material representation of everything that was wrong with the Catholic Church. Destroying images became a means for the laity to display its disapproval of the old church and its support for Reformation.

The iconoclastic rage spread rapidly across Flanders and other provinces. Spontaneous local action was assisted by groups of well-organised exiles, many of whom had been recruited from within the refugee Dutch and Walloon congregations in south-east England and Emden. Some were financed by wealthy Reformed communities in Antwerp. But even where local involvement in iconoclasm was limited, the iconoclasts had at least the passive assent of the anticlerical part of the population. The government in Brussels, however, could hardly claim to have been taken by surprise when the iconoclastic fury exploded. In July 1566, a local government official at Kortrijk had reported to Brussels:

> The audacity of the Calvinist preachers in this area has grown so great in their sermons they admonish the people that it is not enough to remove all idolatry from their hearts; they must also remove it from their sight. Little by little, it seems, they are trying to impress upon their hearers the need to pillage the churches and abolish all images.
> (Parker, 1979, p. 75)

The wave of iconoclasm reached Antwerp on 21/22 August. Watched by large sympathetic crowds who shouted 'Vivent les Gueux' (long live the Beggars), the image-breakers went on to destroy the images in all of Antwerp's forty-two churches, dragging devotional paintings and sculptures into the street where they were smashed to pieces and burnt. This destruction continued well into the night, and two days later the action moved to Zeeland, where the churches of Middelburg and Flushing were pillaged. (Figure 7.5 shows the spread of iconoclasm in 1566.)

The iconoclasm subsequently spread rapidly to the north of the country, where fewer professional image-breakers were involved and the action was less spontaneous. It now became an organised movement, with members of the

Figure 7.5   The movement of the iconoclasm of 1566, from James Tanis and Daniel Horst (1993) *Images of Discord: A Graphic Interpretation of the Opening Decades of the Eighty Years' War*, Michigan: Wm. B. Eerdmans Publishing Co., p. 36

local nobility and civic leaders providing guidance and direction. Thus, when it happened in Leiden and The Hague on 25 September 1566, it took place under the protection of armed nobles and citizens. The Catholic reaction to the destruction of the altars, images and fabric of the old church was largely limited to the southern provinces. In the Walloon town of Lille, where the governor had been so worried about the hedge-preaching and in mid-August had expressed his fear that the iconoclasm might soon engulf his city, the Catholics proved more violent than the Protestants and prevented them from establishing a congregation. But what is truly remarkable is that, with the exception of Gelderland, there was no Catholic opposition to the Calvinist image-breakers. This is even more astonishing considering that the Calvinist revolutionaries constituted a minority. It clearly demonstrated what a determined, ideologically motivated minority could achieve, especially when the local population, as was often the case, associated their actions with those of the confederate nobles or Beggars. But the Beggars had only advocated a halt to religious persecution and the introduction of a toleration of mainstream Protestantism, not an enforced Calvinist reformation of society.

The nobility in the Netherlands had already been split three ways before the outbreak of the iconoclastic disturbances of August and September 1566. A group had remained loyal to Philip II and the government of Margaret of Parma in Brussels; others had joined the confederates around William of Orange and the counts of Egmond and Horn; a third group consisted of militant supporters of Protestantism who were led by Baron Henry of Brederode. Most, however, including some of the more militant supporters of Protestantism, such as Brederode, had been deeply alarmed by the disturbances and violence linked to the iconoclastic fury. They now offered Margaret their support in restoring order if she would allow Protestant worship to continue where it had already been introduced. This compromise was strongly promoted by William of Orange and his supporters, while others under the leadership of Brederode took up a more militant Protestant position. Eventually, by the end of 1566, the compromise position of most of the old confederates had proved untenable and the choice was limited to armed rebellion against Philip II or submission.

By then, Philip II had already decided to use all the force necessary in order to restore the authority of the Catholic Church in the Netherlands. In the autumn of 1566, he informed Pope Pius V that as a good Counter-Reformation ruler he was prepared to take the necessary steps to defend the Catholic Church.

In the end, William of Orange decided to stay on the sidelines of the approaching armed conflict. Instead, Brederode provided the leadership for the armed Protestant rebellion. He managed to generate considerable support for the Reformed cause in Amsterdam and Utrecht in particular. Meanwhile, Margaret of Parma had managed to raise an army and lay siege to the towns of Tournai and Valenciennes, which were controlled by their Reformed communities. By then, Calvinists in the western part of Flanders had joined hands and begun to recruit their own forces. Under the leadership of their ministers, of whom Peter Dathenus and Herman Modet proved particularly important and who were both closely connected with the refugee Dutch/Walloon congregations in England, each congregation had agreed to raise and finance 100 men under its own captain. This was a system that may well have been inspired by the Huguenot churches in France, who had already used an identical system in the Wars of Religion, which had broken out in 1562.

The duke of Alva and the defeat of the rebels

The rebels' campaign proved short-lived. Government forces defeated a rebel army near Antwerp in March 1567. Shortly afterwards, a Reformed force of 3,000 men was totally routed by Margaret's army on their way to relieve their besieged co-religionists in Tournai and Valenciennes. A few days later, the two towns surrendered and the rebellion began to implode. So well before the arrival of the Spanish forces from Italy under the command of the duke of Alva (1507–1582), which Philip II had ordered to go to the Netherlands, the rebellion had come to an end, and with it open adherence to Protestantism. During the spring of 1567, all the recently established Reformed churches dissolved and the ministers fled abroad, from where most of them had come. On 17 April, the magistracy in Amsterdam ordered all Reformed preaching to cease. Shortly afterwards, most of the Reformed leaders left. Brederode sought safety in Emden while William of Orange, who had stayed aloof from the conflict, found it prudent to take up residence in his German estate at Dillenburg.

Margaret and the Brussels government thus managed successfully to defeat the rebels well before the duke of Alva arrived with his 10,000-strong army of mainly Spanish and Neapolitan soldiers in August 1567. Philip II and Alva, however, were determined to use the army they had raised at great cost to make sure that another religious uprising could not occur. Consequently, a policy of suppression and persecution was put in place. Alva had for many years been an advocate of using draconian Counter-Reformation measures against the rebellious Netherlands. He did not wait long to put them into action. As captain-general of Spanish forces in the Netherlands, it was now Alva who held the reins of power in Brussels and not Margaret. On 9 September 1567, after a banquet in Brussels, he had two of the most prominent local nobles, the counts of Egmond and Horn, arrested. They had been among the promoters of the Petition of Compromise in April 1565, but they had never wavered in their Catholicism, and early on in the wake of the iconoclastic disturbances they had offered Margaret their assistance to bring matters under control. Both were convinced they had nothing to fear from Philip II. That proved a grave mistake, for they were tried and found guilty of treason. They were eventually beheaded in the early summer of 1568 in the Grand-Place in Brussels after the execution of another eighteen nobles, among whom were a number of Brederode's collaborators. Margaret of Parma resigned, outraged by Alva's actions, while the executions caused considerable anger within the Netherlands. The events became an important part of the subsequent anti-Spanish propaganda in pamphlets as well as broadsheets.

Before his highly publicised arrest of Egmond and Horn, Alva had already set up his long-planned commission, the Council of Troubles. This Counter-Reformation commission, which was given the task of investigating the preceding two years' disturbances and punishing the guilty, was to prove Alva's main instrument of repression of Protestantism in the Netherlands. By 1569, it had a prosecuting staff of 170 and proved to be highly effective. Some

8,950 people from all sectors of society were investigated and sentenced for either treason or heresy, of whom more than 1,000 were executed during Alva's six-year rule from 1567 to 1573. Most of those affected by the Council of Troubles came from the upper-middle-class layers of urban society, just below the level of the civic leadership. After being hit by condemnations and confiscations, many members of this dynamic mercantile group decided to flee the Netherlands.

EXERCISE

Read Anthology Document 2.23, 'The Council of Troubles in Brill 1566–7', which is an extract from the investigations and convictions of the Council of Troubles in Brill (Den Briel), 20 August 1568. Then answer the following questions:

1   What were the majority of the eighty-three men from in and around Brill convicted of by the Council of Troubles?

2   What were the rest convicted of?

Spend about 20 minutes on this exercise.

SPECIMEN ANSWER

1   Of the eighty-three men who were banished and had their estates confiscated, the overwhelming majority of seventy-nine were convicted of heresy. They were convicted for their involvement in iconoclastic activities, among them the fifty-four unnamed individuals. Others, such as the members of the chamber of rhetoricians, had been engaged in a variety of blasphemous activities, such as mocking the Mass, altars, saints, etc., while some had been actively involved in the Reformed congregations that had briefly come into existence in 1566.

2   The rest, only four, presumably all members of the local nobility, were convicted of treason, having been signatories to the Petition of Compromise and having worn badges and dress showing their association with the Beggars.

The collapse of the hopes and aspirations associated with the 'Wonderyear', followed by defeat and persecution, resulted in a major exodus from the Netherlands. The first wave of refugees left the country in the spring of 1567, when all hopes of some sort of reformation had collapsed. The second wave followed during the winter 1567–68 as a result of the punitive activities of the Council of Troubles. The refugees fled the Low Countries for three main destinations. Those coming from the northern part of Holland, Friesland and Groningen sought safety in neighbouring north-west Germany, especially Emden; those from Brabant, Utrecht and southern Holland fled to Cleves and the German Rhineland; those based in Flanders and Zeeland crossed the sea to England. It has been estimated that around 60,000 people fled the Netherlands in this short period. Even so, many Protestants stayed on and were able to go underground undetected. In places such as Delft, Haarlem and Enkhuizen, Reformed congregations with their own consistories continued to function clandestinely until they could go public again in 1572.

William of Orange and resistance to the Spaniards

William of Orange (Figure 7.6), as we have seen, had been overtaken by events in the 'Wonderyear'. Having taken refuge in his German castle at Dillenburg, he remained on the political sidelines until 1568. He had rejected Brederode's request to join the armed revolt against Spain, but with

Figure 7.6   Hendrik Goltzius, *William of Orange*, 1581, engraving. Photo: © Prentenkabinet, University of Leiden, the Netherlands

Brederode's death and his own condemnation by the Council of Troubles and subsequent confiscation of all his property in the Netherlands, the only option left for him was to replace Brederode as leader of the revolt against Spain.

Initially, William's campaign was one of words. Assisted by skilled propagandists, such as his secretary Philip Marnix of St Aldegonde (1540–1598), who had already (in 1567) published his *True Narration and Apology*, in which he argued that Philip II had violated the privileges and freedom of the seventeen provinces of the Netherlands, William issued a flow of propaganda accusing the Spaniards of unheard of cruelty and maligning Alva in particular. He therefore encouraged his countrymen to take up arms to save their country from being enslaved by the Spaniards.

William's propaganda had a significant impact, not only in the Netherlands, but also among the exile communities of Dutch and Walloons in south-east England and Germany, from where both his army and that of his younger brother Duke Louis of Nassau recruited large numbers of volunteers. Louis's victory in May 1568 at the battle of Heiligerlee proved the exception to the first years of William's armed campaign, and Louis's forces were eventually crushed by Alva a few months later. Meanwhile, however, Louis had managed to establish a rebel naval force while in control of Groningen – the so-called Sea Beggars, who were to play a prominent part in the creation of the Dutch Republic.

Between 1568 and 1572, William of Orange continued the struggle to liberate the Netherlands from Spanish hegemony. Most of his efforts were in the diplomatic field, especially after his failed military excursion into Brabant. William paid particular attention to his contacts with the Huguenot leadership in France and his forces briefly joined the Huguenot campaign in 1569. Increasingly, however, he realised the importance of close cooperation with the leaders of the Dutch and Walloon Reformed churches if the struggle against Spain was to be successful. Thus, when the first national synod of the Dutch Reformed churches met in Emden in 1571, William was represented by his chief adviser, Philip Marnix of St Aldegonde. Marnix had long realised that the support of the Calvinists was essential for a successful outcome of the rebellion, not least for the financial and ideological contribution they were able to make. Marnix therefore worked hard to unify all the Dutch Reformed congregations within and outside the Netherlands into a single body that could act on behalf of all the communities. The synod achieved this objective by establishing an ecclesiastical organisation divided into the three separate provinces of the Netherlands, England and Germany. It was the hardline Calvinists, led by ministers such as Herman Modet and Peter Dathenus, who proved able to determine the outcome of the Emden synod. They made sure that the Reformed churches kept their independence of lay authority. Considering their militancy, it is surprising that they refrained from making any reference to the armed struggle or offering any public support for William of Orange. Perhaps the very different goals of the two groups were too far apart at this time to have made that possible. William's predominantly political objectives of restoring ancient freedoms which, of course, would have meant the halt to religious persecution, did not correspond with the uncompromising Calvinist objective of reforming the whole country along Reformed lines.

The revolt

Most of the war effort against Alva and the Spaniards was conducted at sea by the Sea Beggars. These irregular forces of licensed privateers were based in Emden and the English Channel ports. They were, to a considerable extent, financed by the exiled communities in Germany and England. Despite consisting of a relatively small number of ships, commanded by many of the original confederates or Beggars, they managed to disturb much of the shipping to and from the Netherlands. In April 1572, the Sea Beggars, having been expelled from England by Elizabeth I and from Emden by disaffected local merchants whose trade had suffered as a consequence of their privateering, by a stroke of luck managed to take the town of Brill with a force of only 600 men. This was clearly the good news many among the local population had been waiting for. Subsequently, several towns in Holland and Zeeland rebelled against the duke of Alva. By the end of April, the Sea Beggars controlled or had conquered several towns in Zeeland in particular, such as Flushing, Veere and Arnemuiden. During May, several towns in Holland joined the rebels and further uprisings in the south, in Hainault and Flanders in particular, forced Alva to withdraw from the province of Holland in June in order to regroup his forces. At this point the situation looked precarious for the Spaniards. Much of the country was under rebel control and William of Orange was in the process of raising an army in La Rochelle in France while the Huguenots were poised to lend him military support, now that their forces were idle after the Pacification of St Germain (August 1570). Furthermore, a meeting of the states of Holland in Dort on 19 July 1572 had transformed the rebellion from a movement of armed protest into an alternative government. A new state, the United Provinces, was beginning to take shape. By deciding that William of Orange, as the most prominent member of the states general, should act as protector and head of the Netherlands, a new source of political authority was created, even if at this point it was only recognised by three of the seventeen provinces – Holland, Zeeland and Friesland.

From the summer of 1572, the Calvinists gradually gained control of churches and ecclesiastical property and began to establish proper churches in accordance with what had been decided at the Emden synod. The new consistories, or in several cases the town councils, asked the exiled churches in England and Germany (especially those in London and Emden) to provide them with ministers, since none were available locally. The next decade proved to be an apostolic age for the exiled communities. The larger communities in London and Emden responded by providing around twenty ministers for the 'churches under the cross'. The newly established churches proceeded to create the necessary administrative framework of classes and provincial synods. By

1574, bi-annual synods were in existence across Holland, while the province of Zeeland had to wait until 1579 before a similar set up had been provided, because of the disruptions caused by the war.

EXERCISE

Turn to Anthology Document 2.25, 'Letters to the Dutch Church in London', and read the first letter (a), from the minister Bartholdus Wilhelmi to the Dutch congregation in London, 29 August 1572. How does Bartholdus Wilhelmi portray the situation of the Reformed church in Dort?

Spend about 20 minutes on this exercise.

SPECIMEN ANSWER

Wilhelmi gives a positive impression of the possibilities for the Reformed church in Dort and its vicinity. There was, however, a desperate shortage of ministers. He asked the Dutch church in London to send another four or five ministers to Dort, which was in need of between ten and twelve more ministers. The local governor was very supportive of the Reformation. However, the local population had little or no knowledge of the Reformed religion and practice, and it was therefore imperative for the Dutch community in London to send some of their most experienced ministers and elders.

By late August, the St Bartholomew massacre of French Calvinists guaranteed that the chance of any Huguenot support for the rebellion in the Netherlands had evaporated. Meanwhile, by the end of 1572, Alva had regained full control over most of the provinces, with only the provinces of Holland and Zeeland remaining loyal to William of Orange, but without the backing of the major cities of Amsterdam, Utrecht and Middelburg, who remained loyal to the Brussels government.

Alva used extreme violence to suppress the revolt and went out of his way to emphasise that disloyalty would be brutally punished. The southern town of Mechelen, which surrendered and opened its gates to Alva, was nevertheless sacked by his troops and many of its residents were massacred. This message was quickly digested by many of the southern towns, which subsequently negotiated their surrender and agreed to pay punitive fines. Alva followed the same recipe when he attacked the town of Zutphen and killed hundreds of the town's population of 7,500 (see Figure 7.7). Zutphen's treatment may well have encouraged neighbouring towns in Gelderland to sue for peace, but it was to play a prominent part in the increasingly effective anti-Spanish propaganda.

The next two years proved a difficult period for the rebels and even their hold on the two northern provinces remained precarious. After having taken the town of Naarden and killing its whole population, Alva had moved on to Haarlem, laying siege to the city in late December 1572. Here his army suffered heavy losses during a seven-month siege, while the costs continued to escalate. In July 1573, the city surrendered. By February 1574, the rebels were able to register an important success by forcing the blockaded town of Middelburg to surrender, giving them full control of the province of Zeeland. Meanwhile, Alva had commenced his siege of Leiden, which was to prove one of the longest and the most decisive of the sieges of the revolt.

Den Yſel, bevroſen.

WREEDE MOORT TOT ZUTPHEN

Zutphen beſich met verdragen
Merckten niet de booſe lagen
Van den Spangiaert vol bedroch
T'welck veel lieden heuget noch
Als den Yſel was bevrooren
Wie vermach dit aen te hooren
Sonder weenen, wie ſal niet
Schrickken van dit ſwaer verdriet

10

Uytgetrocken naeckte lieden
Konden niet den Doot ontvlieden
Maer ſy weegens onder ys
Man en Vrou Ionck out en grys
Voor het vriendelyck ontfangen
Wert het ouerſchot gehangen
Staecken Boomen galgen velt
Toonden daer het Spaens gewelt

Don Frederic, Soon van vau den Hartog Alba, d'afgevallene Steden in Over-Yſſel, het Graafſchap Zutphen en daar omtrent, weder verovert en in ſyn magt gekregen hebbende, regt in de Staat Zutphen, een overgroote Moordery en alderhande onmenſchelijke wreetheden aan oeffenende aldaar een ſtraffe, die alle reden en maat te boven ging.

10.

Figure 7.7 *The Slaughter at Zutphen, c.*1620. Part of a series of prints issued under the title *A Mirror of the Spanish Tyranny in the Netherlands*. Photo: © Rijksmuseum, Amsterdam

By August 1574, the defenders of Leiden had no supplies left and the population was starving. William of Orange, who fully recognised the city's strategic and moral importance for the revolt, came up with the idea of opening the dikes, inundating the areas around Leiden, forcing back the Spanish besiegers and making it possible to relieve the city by boat. The scheme appeared to have failed when the relief fleet got stuck halfway between Delft and Leiden because the water level was too low. For weeks the starving defenders could hear the relief fleet firing its guns; then the wind changed and heavy rain raised the water level, making it possible for the supplies and extra troops to get through to Leiden. For the Reformed communities, there was no doubt that this was God's intervention against the forces of Antichrist. Subsequently, the Spanish forces abandoned the siege of Leiden and withdrew from southern Holland, including the cities of Utrecht and Haarlem, which they had conquered at such great cost. Leiden proved a turning point for the rebels, who were now able to consolidate their hold on the provinces of Holland and Zeeland. By then, in the autumn of 1573, Alva had been replaced as governor-general by Luis de Requesens (1528–1576).

In Dutch Reformed mythology, the duke of Alva acquired a special position as the henchman of the pope or Antichrist. By 1569, he was repeatedly depicted as the representative of the Devil and Antichrist in a series of broadsheets (see *Visual Sources Book*, Plates 8.2 and 8.3). As such, Alva had not only enslaved the seventeen provinces (shown as seventeen chained virgins in the broadsheets), but also tortured and murdered those of the Reformed faith (being tortured in the top left-hand corner and hanged in the top right-hand corner) and executed his political opponents (as seen in the beheading of the counts of Egmond and Horn). Alva is shown as sitting on a throne waiting for the Devil to crown him, presumably as king of the Netherlands, while Cardinal Granvelle, who bellows advice in his ear, is offered the papal tiara by the Devil. Evidently Alva was portrayed as an apocalyptic figure who, as some versions of this print stated, served as the rod of God punishing the people of the Netherlands for their sins. This view of the duke of Alva as an instrument of the papal Antichrist proved extremely durable in the revolt, lasting well into the seventeenth century.

The new Calvinist churches

The creation of new Calvinist churches in the north was not without problems. Most town councils sought to keep the new congregations under tight control. In this, they were helped by the fact that they provided salaries for the new Reformed ministers and money for the maintenance of the church buildings. There were clashes between magistracies and ministers, many of whom were hardline Calvinists. The magistracies, for both economic and political reasons, favoured a policy of religious toleration. Often they went to considerable lengths to reassure and protect local Catholics, who continued to constitute a substantial part of the population for decades to come. Prominent Catholics also continued to play a part in urban politics. Thus, ten Catholics remained on the city council in Amsterdam after the city had officially joined William of Orange in 1578 and supposedly been purged of members who did not belong to the Reformed faith.

On top of that there was disagreement about the nature and form of the new Reformed church. Hardline Calvinists favoured a narrow church, restricted to those members who placed themselves under what they termed the discipline of Christ. Only those true members (*lidmaten*) who unquestioningly accepted the discipline of the church could partake in communion. The rest, the majority, were described as sympathisers (*liefhebbers*) and could only attend the sermons. Only after some hesitation did the hardliners accept that the sympathisers could have their children baptised in the Reformed churches. This distinction between a small core of godly members, who were predestined to be saved, and the majority who were less fortunate became an obvious and self-imposed obstacle to growth for the Reformed churches. Recruitment proved slow, and during the 1570s the Reformed churches found it difficult to attract members of the civic elite in significant numbers. This may not have been helped by the fluid political and military situation in the 1570s, when Spanish forces were never far away and full commitment to the Reformed church was far from being without risk. Even after the revolt had gathered substantial ground and the Union of Utrecht had been signed in January 1579 (creating the United Provinces of Holland, Zeeland, Utrecht, Friesland, Gelderland and Ommeland, later joined by Groningen), the Reformed churches only expanded their membership slowly, even if some of the ruling urban elites now began to make an appearance as members and elders. However, it is noteworthy that the hardline Calvinists, despite their unwavering support for the revolt, still received less than wholehearted support from city councils and provincial states. Instead, they continued to favour a policy of toleration towards non-Calvinists, especially Catholics. The religious policy of the government of William of Orange and most of the political leadership remained one of toleration dictated by the political and economic imperatives.

Even after the states of Holland had felt obliged to outlaw the Mass in March 1581, and the United Provinces had finally ousted Philip II as their king by the Act of Abjuration of July 1581, the Reformed churches continued to grow at a slow rate. In 1587, the states of Holland reminded their Reformed ministers that less than 10 per cent of the population belonged to the Reformed faith. In 1615, the grand pensionary of Holland, Johan von Oldenbarnevelt, took the opportunity to inform the English diplomat Dudley Carleton that only a third of the population of the United Provinces were Protestants while Catholics constituted a similar part. The religious landscape of the seven northern provinces that came to make up the Dutch Republic thus remained religiously pluriform in character. Catholicism continued to demonstrate amazing tenacity while Calvinism found expansion beyond a certain level impossible, despite being the official church of the Republic.

Furthermore, from its formative years, the Dutch Reformed church never presented a theologically unified entity. Opinions differed among its leading exponents, especially with regard to the significance of predestination and the need for strict church discipline. A humanist, latitudinarian and tolerant faction, particularly opposed to Calvin's teachings on predestination, which from the 1590s became increasingly associated with the minister and later Leiden professor of theology, Jacob Arminius (1559–1609), continued to play a part in the Reformed church. They became known as Arminians or Remonstrants (so called after the Remonstrance they had drawn up in 1610 after Arminius's death) and soon found themselves engulfed in a growing confrontation with the hardline Calvinists– the Contra-Remonstrants. This eventually resulted in the famous synod of Dort in 1618/19 and the subsequent ejection of the Remonstrants from the Dutch Reformed church. By then, however, the religious issues had become even more irretrievably mixed up with politics. The Arminians had become closely linked with the peace party in the Republic, led by Johan van Oldenbarnevelt, who had secured the Twelve-Year Truce with Spain in 1609, while the hardline Calvinists were associated with the war party led by the stadholder, Maurice of Nassau. The political victory of Maurice of Nassau and the war party in 1619 guaranteed that the war with Spain continued in 1621.

Briefly, however, the possibility of a united and free Netherlands had come close to becoming a reality towards the middle of the 1570s. By then, the political framework had been put in place for the re-formation of the state of the Netherlands. The governor-general, Luis de Requesens, died in March 1576 after only three years in office. Since his replacement was not appointed immediately, his authority reverted to the Council of State in Brussels. The financial problems, already in evidence while Requesens had been in charge, deepened. Unable to pay its Spanish mercenaries, the Council of State was faced with serious mutinies by its own troops, a discontented population and an explosive increase in militant Calvinism in the towns of Brabant and Flanders. By now the revolt, which had hitherto been confined to the northern provinces by Alva and Requesens, had spread to the south, and by the autumn of 1576 it had become a countrywide uprising against Spanish authority. In early November, mutinous Spanish forces stormed Antwerp, then Europe's leading financial and commercial centre, and pillaged the city (see Figures 7.8 and 7.9). News of the 'Spanish Fury' at Antwerp spread quickly across northern Europe, and exaggerated figures for the number of casualties were circulated. The event added further ammunition to the 'Black Legend' of Spanish brutality and became widely used in the anti-Spanish propaganda. These events undoubtedly helped to speed up the negotiations between the rebel provinces and the rest, resulting in the Pacification of Ghent on 8 November 1576. It subordinated all seventeen provinces to the authority of the states general. It stated that a new governor-general should be nominated, provided he would accept the Pacification, and that he should send away the foreign troops and rule solely through natives. Religious matters were to be decided by the states general in due course, while all measures against heretics should be halted.

Figure 7.8   Georg Hogenberg, 'Battle for Antwerp town hall 4 November 1576', copperplate engraving, 20.8 x 27.8 cm, from Michael Aitsinger, *De leone belgico*, Cologne, 1583. Photo: AKG-Images, London

By 1578, however, a new Spanish governor-general, Alexander Farnese (1543–1592), prince of Parma, had been appointed. New resources and troops were added to Philip's war effort in the Netherlands. Under Alexander Farnese's able leadership, a larger and better Spanish army began reconquering the rebel-held towns in the south. With Spanish forces gaining ground, the militancy and fear of the Calvinist-held towns of Flanders and Brabant grew, leaving little room for William of Orange's policy of religious peace between the two main denominations.

<table>
<tr><td>EXERCISE</td><td>Turn to Anthology Document 2.25, 'Letters to the Dutch Church in London', and read the second letter (b), from Daniel de Dieu, 9 August 1582. What, according to de Dieu, was the situation like in the Netherlands and in Brussels in August 1582?

Spend about 20 minutes on this exercise.</td></tr>
<tr><td>SPECIMEN ANSWER</td><td>The overall situation in the Netherlands was bad, according to de Dieu, and the Gospel was far from being universally accepted. There were far too many Catholics or Catholic sympathisers, not to mention atheists and libertines. Even the godly, who had done their utmost to live pious lives, had through their sins added to God's</td></tr>
</table>

Figure 7.9   Franz Hogenberg, 'Spanish atrocities in Antwerp on 4 November 1576', copperplate engraving, from Michael Aitsinger, *De leone belgico*, Cologne, 1583. Photo: AKG-Images, London

anger. This explained to de Dieu how the neighbouring town of Lier could have been betrayed to the Spaniards and many of its inhabitants murdered.

Neither were things going well in Brussels, where the garrison had recently mutinied. This had caused some burghers, both Catholics and Protestants, to arm themselves in order to protect the town hall. Members of the Reformed community had clearly felt exposed in this situation, where some Catholics had tried to encourage the rebellious soldiers to attack them. Rumours appear to have been rife within Brussels about the dangers of attacks from within and without, while the local Catholic population were actively soliciting political support for their cause.

Two years later, when Alexander Farnese had commenced his siege of Brussels, de Dieu informed his friends in London that he had been unable to write to them for some months 'owing to the present critical times' when misery reigned in the city. De Dieu reported that the Catholic majority in the city did their utmost to discourage resistance, pointing out the hopelessness of resistance. Yet there was no need to despair, according to de Dieu, who stated:

> I have no doubt as to the wish of the enemy, but the Lord who formerly protected Israel against the Pharaoh, and us, so long against the Spaniards, still lives in Heaven.
>
> (Cunningham and Grell, 2000, p. 160)

Brussels fell to the Spaniards six months later, by which time nearly the whole of the south had been reconquered by Alexander Farnese. Only the city of Antwerp, by then besieged, and a couple of smaller towns were still holding out. Finally, in August 1585, Antwerp, the commercial capital of Europe, capitulated to Alexander Farnese. As in the case of Brussels, there was no retribution, but Protestants who were unwilling to convert to Catholicism were forced to sell their property and leave the city. Over the next four years, nearly half the city's population of 85,000 people emigrated. They joined a major exodus of up to 150,000 people who left the southern provinces of the Netherlands for the United Provinces in the north and England and Germany.

However, after a difficult decade with significant setbacks and losses, especially in the south, not to mention the murder of William of Orange by a Spanish agent in Delft in July 1584, the United Provinces (or the Dutch Republic, as they became known), were able to consolidate their security and independence from 1588 onwards. By then, what had been a turbulent period had resulted in the formation of a new state. Still, the guidance of the advocate of Holland, Johan von Oldenbarnevelt, who was also the mentor of William's young son and chosen successor, Maurice of Nassau, proved invaluable for providing the young Republic with the necessary stability and security over the next thirty years.

CONCLUSION

This unit is dominated by the theme of religious belief, but economic matters and questions about the legitimacy of leaders were tightly interconnected. The Calvinist Reformation resulted in profound changes to religion and dramatic changes in social behaviour. It also had serious political implications for the city-state of Geneva, both internally and externally.

The Reformation in the Netherlands also shows how the themes are interconnected. Taxation by the government of Philip II was a major point of conflict from the outset and remained so until the late 1580s. Philip's government in Brussels was widely perceived to extort money from the Netherlands without the consent of the local population, thereby violating traditional rights. The armed conflict made matters worse; the duke of Alva introduced many new taxes in order to finance his military campaign in the Netherlands. Where religion provided the primary rationale for flight and emigration, the faltering economy and depressive financial outlook of the urban centres of the southern Netherlands, in particular Antwerp, which had recently become the financial centre of Europe, would have provided enough justification on their own to have encouraged mass emigration from these areas. This, of course, does not even take into consideration the devastation caused by the war nor its costs to the rebels.

To end this unit you will look at the way religious beliefs and economic concerns were brought together in Reformed propaganda.

EXERCISE

Look at the four prints in the *Visual Sources Book*, Plates 8.2–8.5. These were published together (a kind of early modern cartoon) in 1572 at the peak of Alva's reign of terror. Like most of the prints you have encountered in this unit, they are a combination of text and image. Look more closely at Plates 8.4 and 8.5. What do you think the economic message of these prints is?

Spend about 10 minutes on this exercise.

DISCUSSION

The duke of Alva is portrayed as damaging trade and manufacture in the Netherlands.

Plate 8.4 depicts the duke of Alva embracing the Whore of Babylon, typically wearing a papal tiara, identifying the pope with Antichrist. The seven-headed beast is watching from behind Alva's chair. To the left stands an unemployed sailor, while ships with broken masts can be seen lying idle at the quayside and bales of goods lie abandoned. The text explains that ships have fallen into disrepair and seamen are helpless. Merchants are unable to sell their goods (the merchant to the right of the print lifts his arms in despair), while the duke of Alva has his way with the Whore of Babylon. Neither can the peddler (lying at Alva's feet with his basket full of goods) sell his wares, because of Alva's beheadings, taxation and stealing. Plate 8.5 shows Alva devouring a baby, signifying the innocence of his victims, while the corpses of his two most famous victims, the counts of Horn and Egmond, lie beheaded under his feet. Alva is being advised by a three-headed monster wearing cardinals' hats (one of the heads is that of the much-hated Cardinal Granvelle), while a small devil in a monk's habit uses a pair of bellows to fill his head with evil ideas. Alva's financial extortion of the Netherlands is symbolised by the purses he holds in his left hand. The text expands on this by pointing out that Alva has taken the wealth of the Netherlands away by force while murdering innocent people, including Egmond and Horn. This is all lamented by the peasants (the figure to the left of the print, holding a flail) and burghers (the figure to the right, wringing his hands in despair).

In the Reformed propaganda against Alva and Spain, the religious, political and economic arguments were often cleverly mixed together. The message could not be clearer. The economic difficulties encountered by consumers as well as producers were all caused by the duke of Alva. This was yet another way the duke of Alva, acting as the instrument of the papal Antichrist, sought to destroy the godly, Reformed community.

REFERENCES

Benedict, P. (2002) *Christ's Churches Purely Reformed. A Social History of Calvinism*, New Haven/London, Yale University Press.

Cunningham, A. and Grell, O.P. (2000) *The Four Horsemen of the Apocalypse. Religion, War, Famine and Death in Reformation Europe*, Cambridge, Cambridge University Press.

Lindberg, C. (ed.) (2000) *The European Reformations Sourcebook*, Oxford, Blackwell.

Parker, G. (1979) *The Dutch Revolt*, London, Penguin.

Rosemary O'Day

INTRODUCTION

This unit provides a brief introduction to the Reformation in England and Wales. It concentrates on the themes of the formation of the state, and beliefs and ideologies. The principal emphasis is on the Henrician settlement of the 1530s.

You will need to make continual reference to Chapter 3 of the set book by Wallace. This and the Block 2 chronology on the A200 website provide you with a broad narrative structure for your more intensive study of 'episodes' in English Reformation history and attendant debates.

History is about why, not just what. Studies of the English Reformation have, since they began in the sixteenth century itself (with the accounts in John Foxe's *Book of Martyrs* in 1563 and 1570), focused on interpretations and explanations, whether consciously or not, explicitly or implicitly, deliberately or accidentally. The 'English Reformation' is commonly thought to have extended through the reigns of Henry VIII (*1509–1547) and his children – Edward VI (*1547–1553), Mary I (*1553–1558) and Elizabeth I (*1558–1603) – and therefore through much of the sixteenth century. Recent historians have often argued that it was not a single event (i.e. the break with Rome, or the Edwardian settlement, or the Elizabethan settlement) but rather a process for which the people of England had been prepared. Some, however, have disagreed with this interpretation; they have seen the Reformation as a 'supreme event', have sought to restore voluntarism (e.g. it all depended on the personal policies of individuals such as Henry VIII or his minister Thomas Cromwell) and have tried to throw out all ideas that past developments (e.g. Lollardy) had prepared the people to accept Protestantism and the Protestantisation of English life. Whichever interpretation we favour, the reigns of Henry VIII, Edward VI and Elizabeth I seem to mark identifiable stages in this English Reformation. The sections in this unit will home in on three particular phases and show how important historians' 'interpretations' are in guiding us through them. The first phase, the Henrician Reformation, receives most attention.

REIGN OF HENRY VIII

Here are the main issues we will address.

- The break with Rome itself under Henry VIII. Legislating for royal supremacy – who was at the root of it, Henry VIII or Thomas Cromwell? The role of parliament – constitutional implications of the change; whether or not it reflected or was paralleled by a movement for religious reform; to what extent this settlement signified a radical change in the relationship between king and subjects.

- Forces for reformation already present in society and assessment of their importance. To what extent was this a religious reformation? If it was, was this the expression of a popular desire for reform?

EXERCISE

You have read some of Chapter 3 of the set book by Wallace in Unit 6. Now read, and write brief notes on, pp. 106–9, 'Evangelical Reform and the Church of England'

Pick out statements from pp. 106–7 that you think have special relevance for the two themes of this unit.

Spend about 30 minutes on this exercise.

SPECIMEN ANSWER

Relevant statements include:

- the whole of paragraph 1
- 'By 1520 Luther's works had come to England and inspired an early evangelical movement'
- 'In 1529 Henry VIII ... faced a domestic crisis with broad political implications'.

DISCUSSION

Broadly speaking, this whole section is relevant to the two main themes of this unit, so do not worry if the statements you picked out did not match those in the specimen answer. Paragraph 1 neatly sums up the marriage of both themes. The Reformation is seen by some as a political event imposed from above to consolidate the king's authority over his state. It is seen by others as being at least underpinned by deep religious feeling from below.

Between 1529 and 1534, England broke away from papal jurisdiction. This break with Rome and the legislation that surrounded and defined it are often known as 'the official' or 'state' Reformation. This idea in itself poses a question of interest to us as we discuss the state: to what extent was a monarch (the head of the state) able to impose or create a reformation? Was Henry VIII a tyrant who rode roughshod over his people to achieve dynastic stability, or was he a despot who ruled by tacit or overt consent of his people? Or was the official Reformation not the brainchild of Henry himself but rather of Thomas Cromwell, seen by some as the upholder of constitutional, limited monarchy and the disciple of continental Protestantism?

In this unit we are going to concentrate on close reading several Acts of Parliament or statutes. Documents produced by official state institutions (and the processes leading to their creation) have provided crucial evidence for many of the studies of the English Reformation. However, their use poses many technical problems.

EXERCISE

Read Anthology Document 2.13, the Henrician 'Act in Restraint of Appeals to Rome, 1533'. Historians frequently use the evidence supplied by Acts of Parliament to study the growth of the state in England. These Acts are couched in unfamiliar legal language and require close reading if we are to understand them properly. Use the annotations in Anthology Document 2.13 to help you understand what you are reading.

Spend about 60 minutes on this exercise.

> ## Parliament
>
> Parliament, as today, consisted of two houses: the Commons and the Lords. In the Lords sat members of the peerage (nobility) and of the church hierarchy – the lord bishops and, until the Reformation, leading abbots. In the Commons sat representatives of the counties and the boroughs (towns with borough charters from the crown). The process of initiating and passing parliamentary legislation (statute law) developed throughout the period and historians see the Reformation parliament (1529–36) as pivotal to this process.

Answer the following questions in brief note form:

1   What reasons does the Act give for preventing Englishmen appealing to the jurisdiction of the pope in Rome?

2   Does the Act claim that this interpretation of the crown's jurisdiction is new?

SPECIMEN ANSWER

1   Despite the efforts of the king's predecessors to prevent Englishmen appealing to Rome, such appeals have continued and have caused delays, expense and annoyance.

2   No. This is not novel. 'This realm of England is an empire' and this has been established 'by divers sundry old authentic histories and chronicles'.

DISCUSSION

The Henrician settlement was not achieved by a single Act of Parliament but by a number of Acts or statutes. The Act in Restraint of Appeals was placed on the statute book in 1533. It is a very interesting piece of legislation for several reasons. First of all, it makes a bold statement about England's imperial status. England is an empire – an independent state.[1] It explains the relationship between the king and his subjects. The English king governs the realm and has total authority (under God) over it. England is 'governed by one supreme head and king' 'unto whom a body politic, compact of all sorts and degrees of people divided in terms and by names of spiritualty and temporalty, be bounden and owe to bear next to God a natural and humble obedience'. Those subject to the king include both clergy (the spiritual estate) and lay people of all degrees. It also claims that this has long been so – histories have declared and expressed it and it has been accepted by the world. We can imagine Henry's lawyers combing the statute book and the precedents to establish what his predecessors had done to confirm this independence and to prevent Rome interfering with this jurisdiction. (Recall the ways in which late medieval monarchs sought to wrest powers from the papacy.) In early modern times there was no virtue in claiming to be innovative. Henry and his ministers knew that they must appeal to precedent. They cited precedents from the twelfth century onwards. Most important of all, this Act summed up this argument in bold, uncompromising language. Once they had read this preamble, none could doubt what Henry was claiming. The pope's jurisdiction did not extend to England.

---

[1] Note that this meaning of the word 'empire' is different from our common use of the term today to describe the far-flung colonial possessions or areas of influence of a great power.

EXERCISE

Read Anthology Document 2.14(a), the Henrician Act of Supremacy, 1534, and answer the following questions in brief note form.

1 What title did Henry adopt in 1534?

2 By what authority did Henry claim supremacy over the church?

3 How did the Act describe the church?

4 Who shared Henry's supremacy over the church?

Spend about 30 minutes on this exercise.

SPECIMEN ANSWER

1 Supreme Head of the Church of England.

2 He claimed that he derived this authority not from parliament but from convocation (the church's parliament), which had agreed that he held this authority directly from God. Remember that he had used a similar terminology in the Act against appeals.

3 As 'the Church of England'.

4 Henry's rule over the church was shared with no one.

DISCUSSION

The Act is underpinned by the view that the centuries of papal rule had been an illegal usurpation. According to the Act, parliament merely recognised the existence of the sovereign's supremacy and ordered the king's subjects to do likewise. The Catholic Church *in* England is described as the Church *of* England. From being a part it has become a whole, and that whole belongs to England, which in turn belongs to the king of England. Henry's rule was personal and he shared his authority with no one. The king could delegate the powers stemming from this authority to another – as he did when he made Thomas Cromwell his vicar-general – but he did this of his own volition. He has authority to order the church spiritually not only 'to the pleasure of Almighty God, [and] the increase of virtue in Christ's religion' but also for 'the conservation of peace, unity and tranquility of this realm' of England. The jurisdiction of foreigners is rejected outright.

Summary

The Henrician Act of Supremacy confirmed that relations between church and state were now on a new footing. You will recall from Block 1 that English kings had long tried to exert control over church appointments but they had acknowledged, in seeking to come to agreements with the papacy, that such patronage ultimately belonged to the pope. They had also chipped away at the right of literate men to be disciplined only by the church's law (benefit of clergy) while agreeing that true clergy stood outside the king's jurisdiction. Now the crown claimed not only the headship of the English state (and thereby the allegiance as subjects of all its inhabitants, whether religious or secular) but also the headship of the church and its courts. The crown claimed not only the loyalty of the church's personnel but also total jurisdiction over them. (If you have a chance to read the text of the Act in Restrain of Payment of Annates and other Acts reprinted in Elton (1960, pp. 341–73), you will see that other legislation spelt out in detail the extension of the king of England's jurisdiction.)

This is clearly a key legislative stage in the development and definition of the English state.

Who made policy?

The parliament that sat intermittently from 1529 until spring 1536 is known as the Reformation Parliament. Historians, however, debate several issues surrounding it, for example:

- To what extent did it and accompanying legislation represent Henry VIII's own policy, to what extent that of his chief minister, Thomas Cromwell, to what extent that of parliament and to what extent that of the people of England?
- What did it mean in practice?

The first debate may be reduced to a single overarching question: who made policy in the state of England in the early sixteenth century?

English government at the close of the Middle Ages

Before discussing this question with regard to Henry VIII's Act of Supremacy, we need to consider the way in which England was governed at the start of the sixteenth century. Today we are used to interventionist central government, to relatively weak county and town jurisdictions, and to accepting that Britain has a democracy, a parliament and a so-called constitutional monarchy, and, moreover, that these institutions have a lengthy history. At the end of the fifteenth century, things were very different.

England had no written constitution – no single document that spelt out the way in which the government of the state should be organised. The organisation of the central government was in some respects familiar to us: there was a monarch, there was a parliament made up of Houses of Commons and Lords, there was a council (though not a formal privy council), there were central law courts.

England certainly had a parliament to which representatives of the counties (shires) and boroughs (towns with a charter) were sent. These representatives were elected by restricted numbers of voters who at best indirectly represented all the inhabitants, and at worst represented the interests of aristocracy or oligarchs. It was not unheard of for prominent men, such as Richard of York, to pack the parliament. Elections took place during an open ballot and were subject to considerable pressure. Parliament had no acknowledged role in shaping policy. It met infrequently and irregularly at the monarch's behest. It was called mainly to approve taxes and subsidies needed by the crown, although it played a part in laying down laws. Medieval government was not interventionist in the way that modern governments are, and so the number of laws put onto the statute book by parliament was relatively low. Also, it was by no means the only vehicle for making law – the monarch could effectively declare law by proclamation; laws also emerged in the courts through a process of custom, interpretation and precedent.

As for constitutional monarchy, no such concept existed. Certainly there were some restrictions on the power of the monarch. These ranged from those accepted under Magna Carta in 1215, which protected subjects from unlawful arrest and detainment, to the effective removal of whole swathes of life in England from out of the king's jurisdiction by the church of Rome. These apart, English kings were free to make and implement policy in foreign and domestic affairs themselves. In the fifteenth century, the institution of kingship in England was strong.

If you reflect on what you have already read in Block 1, you will note that English kings had devised ways of governing that used the skills of others. There was the king's council, to which were admitted as councillors men (normally aristocrats and leading ecclesiastics) whom the monarch trusted. There was the king's household, in which men employed in apparently domestic roles (such as chamberlain) exerted great influence over the sovereign. There was the court. (The reigns of Edward IV and Henry VII have been seen by some historians as remarkable because of the development of strong monarchical government that built on the institutions of the council and the household to great effect.)

Of course, English kings could not do just as they liked. Otherwise Richard II and Henry VI would never have been deposed. Wise and able kings understood the boundaries. Kings accepted that there were areas into which they must not trespass. Counties, cities, towns and parishes had their jurisdictions. If kings alienated the aristocracy and the commons to an extreme degree, monarchs would be in danger. As was made clear in Block 1, however, there was no room in the English state for constitutional opposition. In order to register grievances, the people first tried a petition; if that failed they had to resort to violence. If they were determined to reject their government, they had no alternative but to depose the monarch.

The royal supremacy

The Act of Supremacy of 1534 removed one of the curbs on the king's, and hence the English state's, jurisdiction over its subjects. From this point, the king visited (inspected) the church either in person or through his vicegerent or through the leading ecclesiastics (archbishops and bishops) who owed their authority to him. Convocation, the 'parliament' of the church, could meet only at the king's summons. Its president under Henry was a lay person – the vicar-general. The clergy were to enforce discipline on the basis of authority derived from the crown and using rules or 'canons' devised by a royal committee. Church courts continued to operate but appeals from them were now not as before to go to Rome but instead to the king in chancery. The crown would issue important dispensations and licences (e.g. allowing a man to be made deacon and priest on the same day), thus controlling an important source of revenue. The crown would not only protect the church's teaching against heresy but would also define church doctrine and, by a set of injunctions, regulate church practices.

If you look closely at the wording of the Act, you will see that it did not pretend to have *made* the king supreme head of the church. Rather it said that the parliamentary statute *confirmed* the existing situation which had been acknowledged by the clergy in their convocation as a grant from God.

It was perfectly natural for contemporaries to assume that this policy and the acts that embodied it were Henry VIII's own creation. There can be little doubt that Henry VIII agreed to it, but did he devise it? Often in the near past it was political or constitutional historians who were most interested in these issues. Geoffrey Elton began by putting forward in 1948 what was then a novel view of the role of Henry VIII in the work of government and in the creation of the Reformation. He believed that Henry was not interested in the day-to-day business of government. He was interested in ends rather than means and Thomas Cromwell, a quiet bureaucrat, took advantage of this fact in order to implement his own reform of government and administration – a revolution in government. The reformation in religion was, according to Elton, part of this process. He produced a large number of scholarly monographs and learned articles elaborating on this position. Nowhere was his challenging view of Henry's part in the Reformation more clearly and persuasively expressed than in a brief pamphlet produced for the Historical Association in 1962, *Henry VIII: An Essay in Revision* (Elton, 1962). In this he dismantled the prevalent view that Henry's reign could be divided into two parts: a period from 1514 to 1529, when Henry allowed Cardinal Thomas Wolsey to govern and served his own apprenticeship, and a period from 1529 onwards, when Henry took up the reins of government and was thus 'the very embodiment of personal monarchy' (Elton, 1962). Elton said that all along Henry had maintained some control over government – for example, throughout the reign he had managed state trials. Elton was, however, most dismissive of the view that Henry was ever totally in control of his government and its policies. Certainly only Henry could make or unmake ministers: both Wolsey and Cromwell were to learn that to their cost. Yet Henry was often manipulated by his counsellors. While it was true that he was diligent in matters of business during Cromwell's ascendancy – reading and signing letters and papers – Elton believed that Henry did not devise and control policy. Henry's actions do not suggest that he had a longstanding plan to break with Rome. He recognised Cromwell's gifts and delegated power to him. Naturally it was a power delegated on condition that Cromwell designed and executed policies broadly to the king's liking. Elton argued that Henry kept a more watchful eye on Cromwell's activities with respect to theological and ecclesiastical affairs. For instance, he took a personal interest in the Act against appeals to Rome in 1533. He rejected the idea, however, that in all matters of moment Henry instructed Cromwell verbally to follow particular courses of action. As most of the business of government was normally carried on away from the court, oral communication between king and minister was impossible, and no letters survive to support this view of affairs.

EXERCISE

Read the short extract from Geoffrey Elton's work below and answer in note form the question that follows it.

> In the hands of Henry VIII personal monarchy did not mean personal attention to the business of government, though it had done so in the hands of Henry VII. Nor did it mean the constant weighing up of conflicting counsel and the pursuit of a personal policy based upon a personal assessment as it did for Elizabeth. It meant the putting of the king's personal force behind policies not of his devising. His greatness lay in the rapid and accurate interpretation of the immediate situation, in a dauntless will, and in his choice of advisers; but not in originality, and it is doubtful if he was the architect of anything, least of all the English Reformation.
>
> (Elton, 1962, p. 27)

How does Elton think that Henry regarded his role as king?

Spend about 10 minutes on this exercise.

SPECIMEN ANSWER

- As a personal monarch who did not concern himself with the minutiae of government but with the broad lines of policy.
- As someone who relied on able counsellors to devise policies.
- He was not a constitutionalist, planning to work with parliament.

DISCUSSION

Elton did see Henry VIII as conducting personal monarchy of a certain kind. Implicitly, Elton also disagreed with the early twentieth-century view that Henry VIII, in legislating for reformation, not only worked with parliament but respected parliament. Elton looked to Thomas Cromwell for the origins of this policy.

In 1503, **Thomas Cromwell** (c.1485–1540) (see Figure 8.1) is known to have been at the Battle of Garigliano in Italy. Thereafter he spent some time as a clerk in Florence and in Antwerp. Between 1510 and 1513, he made a second journey to Italy and had an audience with Pope Julius II, before becoming clerk to a Venetian merchant. He was a lawyer when he became an MP in 1524. In 1525, Cardinal Wolsey appointed him a commissioner to inquire into the smaller monasteries, and in the later 1520s he was Wolsey's secretary. He became a member of Henry VIII's privy council in 1531, Master of the Court of Wards in 1532, Chancellor of the Exchequer in 1533 and king's secretary and Master of the Rolls in 1534. In 1536, as vicar-general, he organised a general visitation of the church and the compilation of *valor ecclesiasticus* (which valued church lands and property for taxation purposes). In 1536, he was the moving spirit in the dissolution of the smaller religious houses and presided over the removal of Queen Anne Boleyn to the Tower. In that year, he was made Henry's Lord Privy Seal and Baron Cromwell of Oakham and in the following year became a Knight of the Garter and dean of Wells. He was interested in humanistic studies and oversaw the printing of the Bible in English in 1539. It was he who negotiated Henry's marriage with Anne of Cleves. In 1540, he was created earl of Essex, but in that same year was executed for treason. In the eyes of some historians, he was the architect of the English Reformation. Some see him as an enthusiast for king-in-parliament. Others see him as an avid Protestant. Still others see him as a capable administrator and secretary.

Figure 8.1   Hans Holbein, the Younger, *Thomas Cromwell*, 1532–33, oil on oak panel, 78.42 x 64.45 cm. The Frick Collection, Henry Clay Frick Bequest, Accssn no. 1915.1.76. Photo: © The Frick Collection, New York

According to Elton, Cromwell was the architect, the builder and the master craftsman of the English Reformation. The king only commissioned the work. Initially Elton ascribed to Cromwell a grand constitutional design. The advent of the 'break with Rome' policy coincided with his appointment to the king's inner council. The concept of England as an 'empire' (a statement of sovereignty) simultaneously joined the field. Cromwell deliberately set parliament upon the pope. He shaped the Act in Restraint of Appeals to Rome, which pronounced the status of England as an empire over which its king was sovereign. 'Cromwell offered to make a reality out of Henry's vague claims to supremacy by evicting the pope from England. To the king this meant a chance of getting his divorce, and a chance of wealth; to Cromwell it meant the chance of reconstructing the body politic' (Elton, 1955, p. 129). Cromwell had in mind a limited constitutional monarchy in which king and parliament worked together. Elton was prepared to accept A.G. Dickens's re-evaluation of Cromwell as a humanist patron of early Protestantism (Dickens, 1959b), but he saw the religious Reformation as essentially a secular political act and not an expression of Cromwell's dislike of Catholicism.

For a time, historians did not challenge the fundamental assumptions on which Elton's case was based. Rather, they studied microscopically the origins of specific pieces of legislation and the procedures surrounding the drafting of bills of parliament (the stage before enactment). But then historians began to realise that Elton's interpretation was as difficult to prove as the one he sought to displace. Joel Hurstfield (1973) tried to come to grips with this issue: was there really a long-term and deliberate Cromwellian plan to locate sovereignty in the king-in-parliament (as Elton thought) or was there a Tudor despotism after all? For those of us who want to know whether the official Reformation was a creature of Henry VIII's will or of the will of Henry VIII *and* his people, this is a crucial question. For those of us seeking to place the Reformation in Cromwell's overall policy, it is no less pressing.

EXERCISE	Read the extract from Hurstfield (1973), 'Was there a Tudor despotism after all?', in the Block 2 secondary sources on the A200 website.
	How does Hurstfield define a despotism?
	Spend about 60 minutes on this exercise.
SPECIMEN ANSWER	Hurstfield defines a despotism in the paragraph beginning 'But first I must define my terms' and ending 'evolution of modern society'. It is an 'authoritarian rule in which the government is resolved to enforce its will on a nation and to suppress all expressions of dissent'.
DISCUSSION	Hurstfield adduced evidence that showed that Cromwell held parliament in contempt. He suggested that the crown wished by the Statute of Proclamations to dispense with the need to work through and with parliament and found evidence that Cromwell had sounded out legal opinions about this. Cromwell wanted simply to use parliament to give authority to the proclamations of the monarch. Hurstfield, writing after the Second World War, thought the situation analogous to 1933 when the Reichstag gave Hitler authority to rule by proclamation. 'But is a thing less tyrannical because it is lawful?' questioned Hurstfield. Was the legislation enacted by the parliament its own legislation or that of the king and his minister? And did parliament in any real sense represent the people?

Despotism or constitutional monarchy?

The debate between Elton and Hurstfield became increasingly acrimonious. Hurstfield's was also a controversial view, which stood outside the predominant Whig tradition that saw English history as developing towards constitutional monarchy. Nineteenth- and twentieth-century historians such as G.M. Trevelyan were in no doubt: 'England was not a despotism. The power of the crown rested not on force but on popular support' (Trevelyan, 1926, pp. 269–70). Elton had gone even further, combining a belief in voluntarism with a belief in progressive constitutionalism:

> Thus the political events and constitutional expansion of the 1530s produced major changes in the position of parliament. Long and frequent sessions, fundamental and far-reaching measures, revolutionary consequences, governmental leadership – all these combined with the Crown's devotion to statute and use of parliament to give that institution a new air, even to change it essentially into its modern form as the supreme and sovereign legislator.
>
> (Elton, 1960, p. 234)

According to Elton, even if England had been a despotism before the Reformation Parliament, it certainly was not after it, and this was all as a result of Cromwell's deliberate policy: 'Cromwell established the reformed state as a limited monarchy and not as a despotism' (Elton, 1955, p. 168). Hurstfield was adamant. Neither Henry nor his minister envisaged a constitutional monarchy. Parliament was used to legislate the secular and spiritual Reformation but it was a decidedly junior partner, and one that was kept well in its place. Parliament was in no sense representative of the people: 'the House of Lords [was] increasingly a pocket borough of the Crown, and the House of Commons [was] elected to a large extent under ministerial and aristocratic patronage.' Parliament did not initiate policy. It did not reach decisions after lengthy free discussions. The monarch and his chief minister kept a firm control over parliament, pulpits and press. Henry and his ministers developed a governmental machine that suppressed dissent, convinced through propaganda that the government's actions were just and right, confirmed the crown's control over foreign policy and religion, seized for the crown enormous emergency powers, and ensured that ministers were accountable to the crown alone. All that Henry did, with or without parliament, was designed to serve one end – the establishment of despotism, the confirmation of his own power (Hurstfield, in the secondary sources on the module website). Elton's study of the enforcement of the Reformation during Cromwell's ascendancy, *Policy and Police*, explored the idea that dissenting opinion was suppressed by a reign of terror that disregarded the bounds of law and humanity. He concluded that the campaign that Henry and Cromwell waged was entirely legal and designed only to convert opinion and achieve stability (Elton, 1972).

Summary

Whether we agree with one historian or another, our conclusions have profound implications for our understanding of the English state at this time and of the role of monarch, chief ministers and parliament within it. This is an interesting example of the difficulty faced by a historian in simply *describing* the government and its machinery. Beyond the bald statement that England possessed a monarchy and certain other institutions (namely parliament, council, central law courts, convocation) everything is a matter of interpretation. The debate could largely be reduced to an argument about the motivation behind the actions of Henry VIII and Cromwell. This is not to say that neither of these historians was speaking the truth as they saw it nor that their work did not deepen our understanding of the processes of government and legislation within this state – both drew on the contemporary evidence at their disposal and interpreted it as fairly as possible. I cannot tell you which interpretation most resembled the true situation. I can only offer my view that Elton overstated his case in an attempt to portray Thomas Cromwell as the instigator of the Tudor revolution in government. By the close of Henry VIII's reign, England's was not a constitutional monarchy and parliament's role was still considerably circumscribed by the crown.

Was the Reformation in sixteenth-century England a popular reformation?

'What Squire Henry wills must be an article of faith for Englishmen, for life or death' wrote Martin Luther. Historians have not all been so certain. Some see the official or state Reformation as running parallel to a popular reformation of belief and practice that lent support to Henry's break with Rome and assertion of royal supremacy. Others think that Henry and his ministers imposed Reformation on the people of England (see Scarisbrick, 1968).

Elton and Hurstfield both saw politics at the centre of the Reformation. Both were political or administrative historians. They had little understanding of the interaction of the socio-economic and religious with the political, and hardly any empathy with the religious feelings that ran on the surface of Tudor society. But is it possible to solve the historical problems surrounding the official Reformation without examining the religious situation? It was here that A.G. Dickens was the pioneer, and it is ironic that his interpretation was to become the centre of one of the most divisive debates in Tudor history and the occasion for a vitriolic attack on him in his obituary! One debate is about causes. One side argued that the advance of Protestantism in England owed everything to official coercion. This view originated in the nineteenth century in a work by Henry Gee, a Roman Catholic historian, and was revived by John Scarisbrick (1968, 1984) and Christopher Haigh (1975, 1993). The other side, led by Dickens, argued that the new religion spread by conversions among the people and that it gained strength independently of the official Reformation. Would the official Reformation have been possible had not a popular reformation underpinned it? This was accompanied by a debate about chronology and the pace of religious change: Dickens believed that Protestantism made early inroads and was a strong force to be reckoned with by 1553, when Mary I came to the throne. Penry Williams (1979), Scarisbrick (1968, 1984) and Haigh (1975, 1993) disagreed and maintained that little of permanence was achieved before Elizabeth's reign.

This exercise asks you about the origins of the Reformation. However, before you consider this aspect further, recapitulate briefly the work you did on the Lollards in Unit 4. Remind yourself who they were, where they were, what they believed and how many of them there were.

Now return to your set book, Wallace, and re-read the paragraph beginning 'Scholars have long assumed....' on p. 107. Then answer the following question:

What are the possible origins of the movement for religious reformation in the early sixteenth century, according to Wallace?

Spend about 20 minutes on this exercise.

According to Wallace, the origins are the Lollard movement and the evangelical movement among ecclesiastics in Cambridge and London, led by William Tyndale.

Wallace dismisses the idea that Lollardy provided the 'social base' for the growth of English Protestantism on the grounds that historians have discovered that the movements were 'discontinuous'. Lollardy had survived only in isolated cells among the rural middle class. He attaches more importance to the influence of Luther's work on the young university churchmen who discussed them in Cambridge and London in the 1520s. This was important in the sense that William Tyndale published an English translation of the New Testament in 1529. On the other hand, until 1529 the religious reformers were suppressed and Tyndale was in exile when he produced this important work.

Wallace does not give references for most of his statements and conclusions in this section. He makes little or no mention of popular enthusiasm for Protestantism thereafter. Read on and you will see that he dissociates Henry VIII from any reform of the church. He credits Archbishop Thomas Cranmer with encouraging preaching based on Biblical texts and closing down pilgrimage centres, thus sparking off the Pilgrimage of Grace. He sees religious reform under the minority rule of Edward VI, Henry's sickly son and heir, as hesitantly begun during the protectorate of the king's uncle, the duke of Somerset, and only vigorously pursued in the final years of the reign owing to the enthusiasm of a few leading churchmen and the radical Protestantism of the duke of Northumberland. The implication of his description is that religious reform was an imposition. Until Henry's death, the only 'clear difference' between the Church of England and the late medieval church in England 'lay in the legal relationship with the papal curia' (p. 108).

The survival of Lollardy into the sixteenth century and its links with evangelical Lutheranism warrants more attention. A.G. Dickens argued that most Englishmen in the early sixteenth century were far less interested in religion than historians have suggested. Few found mysticism attractive. Lollardy had a much wider appeal, especially among the artisans. Dickens showed how Lollardy survived into Tudor Britain and was especially active in the Chilterns, the City of London, Essex, parts of Kent, Newbury, Berkshire, Coventry, the West Midlands, Bristol and the huge diocese of York. As a movement, Lollardy was weak, but the ideas and literature of both Lollardy and Lutheranism were passed along trade routes between Lollard congregations (Dickens, 1959a; 1989, pp. 46–59). J.F. Davis discussed the relationship between heresy and the Reformation in south-east England (Davis, 1983). He showed that there were established Lollard communities in three textile areas in Essex, Kent and London. These areas proved particularly receptive to early Protestantism. Why was this? If you remember what you read of Lollard beliefs, you will readily appreciate that foreign influences tended to reinforce the native traditions of Lollardy – anticlericalism, rejection of the worship of saints, questioning of the sacraments, emphasis on vernacular scriptures, evangelism. In particular instances, therefore, the continuity between Lollardy and Lutheranism seems to have been proven (not rejected as Wallace claims).

This receptiveness to Protestantism was, however, highly localised. Lancashire, for instance, remained resistant to Protestantism until the seventeenth century. This was probably partly owing to the isolation of the county, which until the mid sixteenth century had no trade links with London and the south-east. Partly it is to be explained by the fact that the local clergy remained unconverted – attempts to impose Protestantism were spearheaded instead by university-trained theologians rather than local laity and clergy. Historians have been quick to note that the areas in which Lutheranism made most headway tended to be the capital, ports (such as Hull and Bristol) and university towns – towns and cities exposed to European influences.

The idea that anticlericalism was rife in early sixteenth-century England has also been a subject of disagreement. Christopher Haigh contended that anticlericalism as a concept was almost unknown until later in the century (Haigh, 1983). People attacked individual priests for their parasitism but they had no quarrel with the idea of a clergy mediating between them and God. In some ways, this is a persuasive argument: even after the Reformation the man on the proverbial cowpath probably found the behaviour of the parish priest he knew far more interesting than any abstract idea. Equally, though, is it not probable that the behaviour of this same priest coloured his view of the institution of priesthood as a whole? Did not contemporaries move from the particular to the general? Certainly one cannot deny that anticlericalism ran through the thoughts of early Tudor intellectuals, nor that early radical reformers such as John Hooper found it difficult to reconcile the concept of a clergy with their extreme primitivism and belief in the priesthood of all believers. Haigh's is perhaps an entirely academic argument. Whether one accepts that there was no early opposition to a clergy or not, it seems abundantly true that criticism of deplorable aspects of the behaviour of both regular (monks, nuns, friars) and secular (deacons and priests) clergy did *predispose* the laity in favour of radical correction of such abuses and that a reading of the Scriptures led at least some to question the primitive origins of the priesthood.

Historians who emphasise the swell of popular discontent with late medieval religion tend to reject the idea that the Henrician and later reformations were imposed on the English people as a result of the will of either the monarch or his/her chief ministers. The converse is true of historians who favour voluntaristic interpretations and believe that the condition of the medieval church was less dire than historians from a Protestant tradition have suggested and that the people in general were highly supportive of it. John Scarisbrick's *The Reformation and the English People* (1984) revived this interpretation:

> The English Reformation was only in a limited sense popular and from below. To speak of a rising groundswell of lay discontent with the old order, of growing 'spiritual thirst' during the later Middle Ages, and of a momentous alliance between the crown and disenchanted lay folk that led to the repudiation of Rome and the humbling of the clerical estate is to employ metaphors for which there is not much evidence.
>
> (Scarisbrick, 1984, p.1)

Some of the evidence that Scarisbrick and others adduced to rehabilitate the late medieval church and the religious devotion of lay people within it is interesting and often convincing, but unfortunately his attack has little power behind it. He aims his punches largely at straw men. The reader searches in vain for any statements from historians such as Dickens (1989), Claire Cross (1976) and C.S.L. Davies (1976) that indicate that the Reformation did come from below in the sense that Scarisbrick (1968, 1984) and Haigh attack. They perhaps stress the factors which favoured the acceptance of a break from Rome and of Protestantism and those which provided a continuous tradition of radical critique of the church, but they nowhere state or imply that all English people wanted reformation, either before or after Henry's legislative extravaganza.

This overstatement of the case is unfortunate because the research accomplished into the religion of the laity was extremely valuable. Scarisbrick counters the argument that the Reformation represented the triumph of the discontented laity with a detailed picture of lay participation in the pre-Reformation decades that enriches our understanding of the reception of the Reformation. Scarisbrick's medieval lay person was not a second-class citizen, oppressed and put upon. He or she was a partner in religious life. Although not permitted an active role in public worship, the laity was intimately involved in the church's liturgical life and in the communal life of the local church. Parish fraternities were studied to support this view. Wills were combed to show the religious views and the charitable bequests of lay men and women. Historians writing in the 1990s went on to elaborate on this picture of the vitality of late medieval religious life. Eamon Duffy's *The Stripping of the Altars* (1992) and *The Voices of Morebath* (2001) captured the public imagination with their vigorous documentation of lay religion at community level.

EXERCISE

Revisit the work you did on the DVD in connection with Unit 4. Then turn to your Anthology Documents 1.30a and 1.30b. How far do these items assist us in understanding popular religion in early sixteenth-century England?

Spend about 20 minutes on this exercise.

The items indicate that some lay people were actively involved with the church at parish and community level. The calendar of the church's year also determined the community and the social year, providing everything from entertainment to education. The items provide details of such activities and as such are highly valuable. However, none of this documentation addresses either the extent to which the laity were involved in religion (e.g. how many made gifts to their local church) or the depth of their religious understanding and faith.

Clearly, in the early sixteenth century there were pious lay people, and ordinary laity were involved at some level or another in the wider life of the church. If, however, historians concentrate exclusively on this involvement, they do miss much evidence to the contrary. Also, even the evidence of attachment to the old church may be interpreted in several ways.

When, for example, we note the furious response of the laity to attacks on 'their' parish churches that developed into the Pilgrimage of Grace in 1536, it was a fury that officials were removing gifts parishioners and their ancestors had made in memory of loved ones and not necessarily a fury at the sacrilege that underlay the attack. The work of W.K. Jordan, moreover, suggests that lay bequests of masses for the dead were in marked decline in some but by no means all counties at the start of the sixteenth century (Jordan, 1961).

Summary

Historians disagree about the extent to which there was popular enthusiasm for reformation during Henry VIII's and Edward VI's reigns. It is important to note the links between early Protestantism and surviving Lollardy in parts of the country. Conversely, it is also important to note that there is evidence of considerable lay piety within Catholicism. Especially noteworthy are the sources that historians have used to support their various interpretations – wills, court records, church accounts, church fabric and furnishings, and works of religious art among them.

Crown and court

There is evidence of the spread of Protestantism early at court and among some leading ecclesiastics. Some of these 'converts' were bound to Protestantism, at least partially because of their political dependence upon the official break from Rome – for example, Thomas Cromwell, Henry's chief minister, Thomas Cranmer, archbishop of Canterbury, and Anne Boleyn (see Figure 8.2), the king's second wife, who has been seen by some as the 'cause' of the Reformation. Lutheranism did take root at court nonetheless and those who were attracted to evangelicalism had to tread warily with the king.

Figure 8.2 Hans Holbein, the Younger, *Anne Boleyn*, sixteenth century, oil on canvas, 29.5 x 34.5 cm. Hever Castle, Kent, UK. Photo: The Bridgeman Art Library, London

What was Henry's own position? Did he really see the Reformation as entirely a matter of asserting the royal authority vis-à-vis papal claims? There is debate among historians about Henry's personal attitude to the new religion. Some argue that Henry remained a Catholic in most matters of faith until his death. There were periods during the later part of his reign when the lead of conservative Catholic ministers and churchmen was followed. He divorced Anne of Cleves, had Cromwell executed, had parliament pass the repressive Act of Six Articles, which condemned Protestant heresies, and objected to the English Bible that Cromwell had supported in 1539. Yet it is also true that Henry did not enforce the Six Articles, allowed the middling sort access to the vernacular Bible in 1543, left Cranmer in office, added rituals such as creeping

Henry VIII's queens, humanism and Protestantism

Catharine of Aragon had received a humanist education in a country where women had a history of acting as regents. In England she was an enthusiastic supporter of the New Learning and brought the humanist scholar Juan Luis Vives over to educate her daughter Princess Mary (later Mary I). Her humanism was accompanied by pious Catholicism.

Two of Henry's queens were, however, closely associated both with humanism and with the advance of Protestantism at his court. Anne Boleyn is in the popular imagination more typically seen as a 'tease' who bewitched the king and 'caused' the break with Rome. Yet there was a very different side to her. As early as 1530 she was noted for her piety and her interest in French humanism. As queen, she was an important patron of humanist scholars, and possessed a reputation for favouring the vernacular Scriptures. There were discussions of the English Bible at her table in the king's presence. She ordered her ladies-in-waiting to wear girdle books (like those you can see in Figure 8.3 and in the *Visual Sources Book*, Plate 7.1) about their waists for use in devotion. One of these contained a prayer thanking Henry for giving the Scriptures to the people (see the *Visual Sources Book*, Plate 7.2 for the frontispiece to a Bible showing Henry doing just that – this image also appears on the module website for closer inspection). It was an idea that his daughter Elizabeth copied (see the *Visual Sources Book*, Plate 7.3). At her death, Anne charged the care of her infant daughter Elizabeth to Matthew Parker (see Figure 8.4), her humanist chaplain (and Elizabeth I's first archbishop of Canterbury).

Catherine Parr (see Figure 8.5), Henry's sixth wife, to whom he was still married when he died, by contrast had not received a humanist education. Rather, she wrote that she had 'no curious learning ... but a simple love and earnest zeal to the truth, inspired of God'. When she wed Henry, however, she began a humanist education, learning Latin and practising italic handwriting. She wrote two works of her own, the Lutheran *Lamentations* and the *Prayers or Meditations* based on Erasmus and Thomas à Kempis (for a handwritten book of the *Prayers*, see the *Visual Sources Book*, Plate 7.4) Her chaplains were noted Protestant humanists and her ladies also were often pious and learned. Historians debate the extent to which both queens became the focus of Protestantism as well as humanism at court.

to the cross to the list of banned ceremonies, confided his precious son's upbringing to noted Protestant humanists Sir John Cheke, Dr Richard Cox and Sir Anthony Coke, ordered Cranmer to provide a critique of Catholic service books in 1544, proposed replacement of the Mass by a communion service in 1546, and favoured the Protestant Edward Somerset, earl of Hertford, and John Dudley at his court. It is possible, however, to see his flirtations with both sides (conservative and evangelical) as part of political and diplomatic games. For instance, the proposal to replace the Mass was part of an outrageous suggestion Henry made to the French Admiral d'Annebault in August 1546 that England and France should both convert the Mass into a communion,

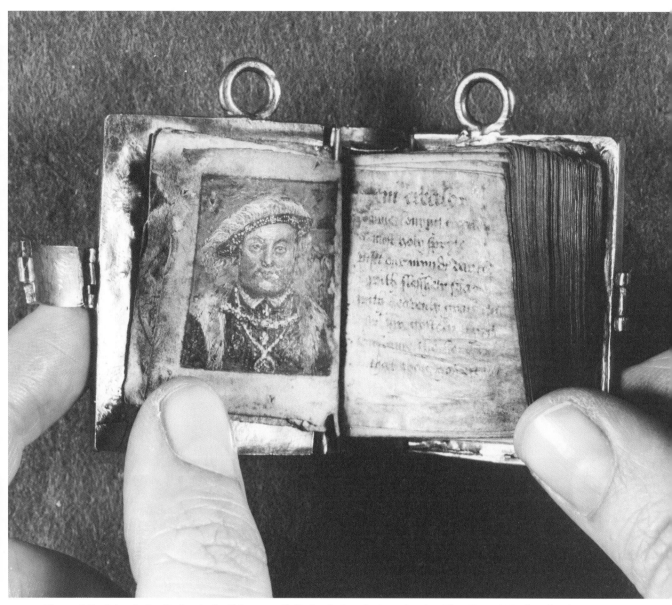

Figure 8.3   John Croke, Psalms in English verse, Girdle book: frontispiece showing King Henry VIII of England, *c*.1540. This demonstrates the prominence given in works of devotion to Henry VIII as head of the English church. It also shows the extremely small size of some of these books. Photo: © The British Library, London

break with Rome and threaten to break with the Holy Roman Emperor if he did not do likewise. Cheke, Cox and Coke were not Protestants at the time – they were Christian humanists (just as Sir Thomas More had been, see Figure 8.6) – and the content of Edward's education was humanist and not Protestant. Hertford and Dudley were made much of at court because of their ability and loyalty, and not because of their Protestantism.

Some historians emphasise discontent with the Catholic Church, others emphasise content, but the question is surely one of the balance between these

Figure 8.4 Matthew Parker, *Remigius Hogenbergh*, published 1572, engraving, 10.9 x. 8.5 cm. Note the simple attire of this archbishop. Photo: © National Portrait Gallery, London

Figure 8.5 Unknown artist, *Catherine Parr*, *c.*1545, oil on panel, 63.5 x 50.8 cm. Photo: © National Portrait Gallery, London

forces. It is also one of influence, leadership and power. None of these historians are able to *quantify* their assertions. Even if such were possible, it is far from clear that the case would be proven by superiority of numbers. Perhaps, for example, it is true that discontent, over and above a certain level, is more potent than content – especially, or perhaps only, when given strong leadership from above. Or perhaps we could posit that those who were discontented with medieval Catholicism, no matter how 'wrong' they may have been, were in some way more influential than those who were happy – they were the intellectuals, the aspiring gentry and bureaucrats, the reforming spirits and, by the very nature of things, were more aggressive than those who approved the status quo or wanted internal church reform. In other words, cadres were decisive.

Figure 8.6   Hans Holbein, the Younger, *Thomas More and his family*, 1527. Sir Thomas More, Henry VIII's lord chancellor, was a noted humanist scholar. His refusal to accept Henry as head of the Church of England and the monarch's divorce from Catharine of Aragon was a major blow to the king and resulted in More's trial and execution. Pen and brushwork, black and brown ink over a chalk drawing, 38.9 x 52.4 cm. Kunstmuseum Basel. Photo: © Martin Bühler/ Kunstmuseum Basel

The historian seeking to determine whether the climate was favourable for a religious reformation perhaps needs to look not at relative content or discontent with the church in numerical terms, nor at the merits of the case against that church, but rather at who was discontented and how they displayed their unease. All the historians arguing over this could well be 'right'. Yes, the majority of the people were used to Catholicism, and were willing to live with it and participate in it on its own terms, even to enthuse about it. Nevertheless, there were significant pockets of discontent at popular level that provided those springboards for early Protestantism. There were traditions of anticlericalism, antipapalism and veneration for the Scriptures that helped Protestantism make headway. Most important of all, there were numbers of very influential men and women, extremely vociferous individuals, who criticised the Catholic Church.

CONTINUING REFORMATION UNDER THE CHILDREN OF HENRY VIII

EXERCISE

Read and make brief notes on the section 'Elizabethan church settlement and civil war' in the set book by Wallace pp. 133–9.

Look back at p. 108 of your set book and you will note that Wallace believes that little or nothing about the Church of England had changed by Henry's death in 1547, apart from the break with Rome. Historians have lately been preoccupied with the question of the conversion of the realm to Protestantism. Work in this area covers the reigns of all of Henry VIII's children and, indeed, those of the Stuart monarchs who succeeded them in the seventeenth century. This has come to be known as the continuing Reformation. How speedily did Protestantism take hold? What factors either facilitated or impeded its progress? See if you can find Wallace's view of when England was converted to Protestantism.

Spend about 15 minutes on this exercise.

SPECIMEN ANSWER   Wallace dismisses the idea that Protestantisation occurred before the late sixteenth century and believes that even in Elizabeth's reign it was gradual: 'her [Elizabeth I's] reign saw the gradual Protestantization of English religious life'.

DISCUSSION   Because Wallace is providing a narrative account of European Reformation over a broad geographical area and a very long chronological period, there is inevitably a tendency to summarise. There is little or no room for discussions of interpretations and debates. Instead, there are often bald assertions about what did or did not happen and why. As a result, you are often being presented with the author's conclusions about a debate – as with his view that Protestantisation awaited the reigns of Elizabeth and the early Stuarts. Our earlier work in this unit has shown that while historians often agree about some basic facts (e.g. the date of an Act of Parliament) they frequently disagree fundamentally about another kind of fact (whether the Henrician settlement was an official reformation only, for example.) The set book obscures this uncertainty. It is useful, indeed necessary, to read such accounts, but we have to be aware of their limitations. We need to delve deeper into the primary evidence and the work of historians based on this.

How rapidly did Protestantism spread? Those who argue that there was a rapid religious reformation built on Lollard survivals and religious discontent often overstate their case. There is a tendency to assume that the heresy cases that came to light were more representative than they in fact were, to overemphasise the importance of the Lollard tradition. Yet those who assert that Protestantisation did not occur until the second half of the century often fail to criticise their sources adequately. For example, it is unsurprising in an age of poor record keeping and poor survival of episcopal court books that there was not much recorded heresy under Mary.

Historians have tried to end the argument once and for all by studying local records. The pre-Reformation diocese of Lincoln was enormous: it covered nine midland counties (Bowker, 1981). It was relatively well administered. In theory, one might have expected that the Reformation would have come early to such a diocese: there was a university (Oxford); there were important towns; there was an area of strong Lollard influence. Yet it has been cited as a classic example of slow reformation from below. Its bishop, John Longland, was a vigorous but conservative man. He held regular visitations of the diocese and rooted out Protestantism whenever he came across it. The clergy and the laity showed little inclination towards Protestantism until the late 1540s, and effective evangelisation came only in the reign of Elizabeth. Unfortunately, the documentation to prove such allegations is thin on the ground. The court book recounting Longland's persecution of the Buckinghamshire Lollards is missing. Court records of any kind are few. The author of the major study of this diocese is cautious: 'in 1529, in the diocese of Lincoln, all our evidence suggests that heresy was confined to the Chiltern area, at most fifty miles square, and to a few young scholars in the University of Oxford' (Bowker, 1981, p. 64). In other words, documents provide one kind of evidence but the absence of documentation provides another.

A study of Tudor Lancashire drew bolder conclusions. There was a revival of traditional Catholicism in this county prior to the 1520s, and this meant that the people had little quarrel with the Catholic Church and resisted the Reformation.

> The fairly intensive efforts at conversion made in the reign of Edward had reaped only a meagre harvest, and Protestantism had gained very little support by 1559. Though habits of church attendance [enforced by the strict laws against resistance] might give the Elizabethan Church a period of grace in which Catholic opinion could be attacked and a reformed theology promulgated, success would only be achieved by a sustained campaign of propaganda and coercion.
>
> (Haigh, 1975, p. 225)

This was difficult in an impoverished and remote county with weak institutions, poorly educated clergy and unsympathetic officials and gentry.

Studies of Northamptonshire (Sheils, 1976, 1979), Cambridgeshire (Spufford, 1974) and Sussex (Lander, 1976) echo the view that Protestantism had made little headway before Elizabeth's reign, but they often emphasise that there were marked local variations. For example, a study of three villages in Cambridgeshire showed that one, Willingham, had a secret Protestant conventicle (meeting), an enthusiastic Protestant congregation thereafter, anti-episcopalian spokesmen in the 1630s and, afterwards, a thriving Congregationalist church, whereas Dry Drayton remained resistant to Protestantism, despite having the prominent evangelist Richard Greenham as its minister for twenty years (Spufford, 1974). Similarly, Protestantism thrived around Lewes but not in much of the rest of Sussex.

Probably regional studies have too coarse a mesh to be of great value in charting and explaining popular reactions to the new religion. Within any given region, diocese or county there was a variety of religious response. Instead, it is important to move forward and study localities where the loyalty of the people might be swayed by individuals, local interests, patronage, the position of the local magnate, social considerations and economic conditions. Micro-studies have become extremely fashionable. While overmuch emphasis on the individual community has disadvantages, such studies do enable the historian to draw a nuanced picture of religious life in the sixteenth and seventeenth centuries.

When you are considering the value of any particular historical work, you will wonder what contemporary evidence the author has used and whether they used it intelligently.

Upon what kinds of primary evidence have historians drawn? Historians have displayed considerable ingenuity in their use of sources. Among these, ecclesiastical court records have been important sources of information. (You have used early examples of these for your study of the Lollards in Unit 4.) In addition, the preambles (opening clauses) of wills have been used to chart popular religious beliefs and changes therein, and wills themselves have been used to show the types of religious and charitable bequests made by individuals.

EXERCISE

Read Anthology Document 2.15, 'Preambles to wills as indicators of religious belief'.

Compare and contrast briefly the contents of the first paragraph of each of the first two wills. Please note that the information given in the document headings was extracted from the preambles of the wills themselves. What are the features they have in common? What differences do you note?

Spend about 20 minutes on this exercise.

SPECIMEN ANSWER

Each of the wills begins with a statement of the identity of the testator and the date the will was made. Usually the will contains a note of the testator's status and/or occupation and place of domicile. This is followed by a bequest of the individual's soul to Almighty God. Sometimes this is quite elaborate, amounting to a statement of beliefs about God and salvation. It is here that there are very noticeable and important differences.

DISCUSSION

Even contemporaries employed the preambles of wills as evidence of people's religious beliefs. In 1532, the corpse of a Gloucestershire man was disinterred and burned as a heretic by order of convocation because in his will he denied the mediation of the saints as part of the way to salvation. When local church records (including wills) and the wills held by the Prerogative Court of Canterbury were opened to the public in the 1950s, historians fell upon this new source with enthusiasm. They were the answer – by counting the number of 'Protestant' or 'Catholic' declarations historians would be able to determine the extent to which English people were converted and the pace at which they were won over or not. Most studies showed a decrease in the number of traditionalist formulae over time and a commensurate increase in the number of reformist or committed Protestant formulae. Was it wise to use wills in this way?

Wills were usually written not by the testator him- or herself but by a professional scrivener (writer) or the local clergyman. The scriveners used standardised preambles (Spufford, 1971). Local clergymen were called in to the testator who had not already made a will to record their dying wishes but, faced by the sick and weak, probably penned the preamble that most closely voiced their own religious beliefs rather than those of the dying person. Ill-advised use of unconventional or unorthodox formulae might land those testators who were not on their deathbeds before the ecclesiastical courts.

Possibly only the most idiosyncratic of wills – those characterised by strongly individual phraseology – reflected an individual testator's personal beliefs. Will preambles *cannot* be used safely statistically to record the exact religious affiliations of the population or changes in that affiliation (Spufford, 1974, p. 334).

Are wills, therefore, useless to the historian? No, they may be used to indicate general trends. It is simply that they have to be used with care and discrimination, and that the results have to be explained. It seems safe to assume that the residual tendency was that of conservatism and conformity. We would expect that it took an effort of will (and some courage) to write a decidedly Protestant testament when the establishment was Catholic, and vice versa. Probably only a progressive would use the services of a Protestant scribe and traditionalists and Catholics would decline to do so. In this way, a long run of wills analysed statistically will reveal a percentage of enthusiastic and committed Protestants and Catholics in a reasonably reliable fashion.

Non-traditional will formulae seem to have been increasing from the late 1530s onwards. In Kent this was noticeable from 1538 and in East Sussex from the mid-1540s (Clark, 1977, Mahew, 1983). Unsurprisingly, this tendency gathered momentum under Edward VI, when there were official attempts to convert the population to Protestantism. Under Mary, however, when one might have anticipated a sharp swing back to traditional formulae, the percentage in East Sussex only reverted to 50 per cent of the Henrician rate. Protestant wills in East Sussex remained at 10 per cent until Elizabeth ascended the throne in 1558 and traditionalist wills never accounted for more than 50 per cent of the total. At Elizabeth's accession, traditional preambles fell to 19 per cent of the total, only slightly higher than the percentage of openly Protestant preambles. Even in Yorkshire, non-traditional formulae were in the majority after 1549, with the exception of the city of York, which long remained conservative. A smaller sample of wills from the diocese of Peterborough suggests a similar pattern and indicates that at the start of Elizabeth's reign, before the Protestant future was assured, 5 per cent of wills were distinctly Protestant in terminology and 25 per cent were neutral. Protestantism showed itself in Norwich wills from 1535 onwards and seems to have been so entrenched by the end of Edward's reign that Mary I was unable to reverse the tide. Work done by Scarisbrick (1984) on the basis of 2,500 wills and by Claire Cross (1982) for Hull and Leeds indicated the traditionalism of the majority of testators. These results suggest the sorts of local variation that our earlier discussions would lead us to expect. They indicate that, while to some extent testators or their scribes did play safe, there were still committed Protestants in some parts of Marian England and still traditionalists and Catholics in Edwardian and Elizabethan England. Local knowledge can help to explain these variations.

Protestantism had certainly made substantial inroads, especially in given regions and communities, before 1558, and the extent of this Protestantism is underestimated if we merely count martyrs or near martyrs. Circumstantial evidence also points in this direction. Wills were made by many of those with property. In general, they represent the older generations and male heads of household. If we accept with Susan Brigden that Protestantism had its greatest appeal for youth and women (Brigden, 1989), then we would expect that there would be an inbuilt bias against Protestantism in any sample of wills before 1560. Similarly, if we accept that Protestantism was at its strongest among those groups who had been open to Lollard influence – artisans, shopkeepers, lower clergy – then we would again expect that any will sample would under-represent Protestantism because wills over-represented the better-off elements of society. John Fines's index of 3,000 known Protestants between 1520 and 1558 shows a preponderance of workers among the early Protestants, which may have been obscured by the amount of attention historians have always given to the network of Marian exiles, which was dominated by clergy, intellectuals and merchants.

This demonstrates several points. First, when a new source is exploited by historians, its advantages are often unintentionally overplayed. Then what is called source criticism takes over. Does the evidence really 'say' what historians have said it says or not? Second, source criticism is an extremely important part of 'doing history'. It involves finding out how and why the records were compiled in the first place – who wrote them, when did they write them, who did they target them at, what was their motivation? Sometimes this is called investigating their provenance. This can often seem a rather negative activity, but it does have positive advantages. Above all it enables us to comment on the meaning and importance of statistics. It means that we come much closer to an understanding of the complexity of the issues we raise about the past.

Reign of Edward VI

EXERCISE

Re-read the paragraph beginning 'Henry's sickly successor' on p. 108 of the set book by Wallace. There were determined attempts under Edward to evangelise England. These occurred in two phases. Can you suggest what these were?

Spend about 10 minutes on this exercise.

SPECIMEN ANSWER

They were (i) a phase of cautious and gradual reform under the protector, the duke of Somerset (Edward Seymour, formerly earl of Hertford, uncle of Edward) and (ii) a much more radical phase under his successor, John Dudley, duke of Northumberland.

DISCUSSION

It is clear that Protestants were in the ascendant at court and in the church hierarchy during Edward's reign. If bishops such as Longland had had a conservative impact under Henry, then new appointments such as those of Nicholas Ridley, Hugh Latimer and John Hooper to the episcopate under Edward certainly tried to reverse the trend. These bishops had an uphill struggle. The limited records that survive for this period show that the ministers were ignorant of the Scriptures and of the church's teaching, and that the people still followed the traditional ways.

Each of these phases was marked by changes in the liturgy (including offering both bread and wine to lay people at the communion)[2] and the introduction of two new books of common prayer. The first, introduced in 1549, was in English but was largely based on the Catholic Mass book. It was produced by a committee of divines headed by Thomas Cranmer, archbishop of Canterbury. The prayer book of 1552 was more radical and included the Act of Uniformity and the famous Black Rubric, which explained why communicants should kneel to take the sacrament.

EXERCISE

Read the extract from the Preface to the Edwardian Book of Common Prayer, 1552 (Anthology Document 2.16(b), paragraphs 1–6). What are the changes that it identifies in common prayers in the Church of England?

Spend about 30 minutes on this exercise.

SPECIMEN ANSWER

- It claims that the original divine service has been corrupted.
- Common prayer was ordained to lead to an increase in godliness but over time this intent has ceased to be fulfilled.
- Originally the Bible was to be read through once during each year and be meditated upon by the clergy so that people knew and could defend the doctrine of the church.
- People would also be inspired thereby to live Godly lives.
- Over the years, myths and legends have been introduced and Bible readings neglected.
- Whereas in the early church the people would have heard the Bible in their vernacular tongue 'the service in this Church of England ... hath been read in Latin to the people, which they understood not ...'.

DISCUSSION

The wording quoted in the bullet point above is similar to the wording in the 1549 Book of Common Prayer: 'the service in this church of England (these many years) hath been read in Latin to the people which they understood not; so that they have heard with their ears only; and their hearts, spirit and mind, have not been edified thereby'.

EXERCISE

Now read the extracts from the communion service in the two Edwardian prayer books. Read all of 2.16(a) (paras 1–18) and paras 12–23 in 2.16(b), paying particular attention to the instructions given in bold. (Use the annotation in the anthology to help you with the archaic language.)

What do the instructions tell you about the nature of worship?

Spend about 45 minutes on this exercise.

DISCUSSION

This is a difficult exercise and for that reason I am proceeding directly to a discussion, rather than giving a specimen answer. If you managed to make some of these points, then well done.

Both extracts provide for an abbreviated service, without celebration of the communion, if there are not sufficient people present to participate (see 1549, para. 13; 1552, para. 19). This was aimed at stopping what was considered to be a

---

[2] Prior to this, lay people had partaken only of the consecrated bread at communion, although wine was offered to them at the absolution of sins. Some historians have ingeniously used records of the amounts of wine consumed to calculate the numbers of parishioners attending Sunday services.

superstitious practice – a mass sung not to bring grace to the communicants but rather for the dead. The second prayer book is much more blunt about this instruction and specifies that there must be lay people present to hold a communion (see 1552, para. 20). The first prayer book, published at a time when there still were chantry chapels in which masses were said for the dead, gave detailed instructions for masses within them. The second prayer book, published after the dissolution of the chantries, made no reference to them.

The first prayer book ordered that the communion bread should be 'unleavened and round' (1549, para. 14). The second prayer book ordered that it should be 'the best and purest wheat bread' (1552, para. 21). Both prayer books struck at another practice – that of secreting away the bread (which was considered to be the body of Christ) for 'superstition and wickedness'. The first prayer book ordered that the bread should be placed in the communicant's mouth so that he or she could not drop it or take it away with them (see 1549, para. 18). The second prayer book changed this (the bread would be given to the communicant's hands (1552, para. 16)) but insisted that all remaining bread and wine should be consumed by the curate (see 1552, para. 21). Both prayer books ordered that the parishioners should be responsible on a house-by-house basis for paying for the bread and wine. The first prayer book would have this achieved through the offertory plate at the communion, the second by a household levy every Sunday.

Both prayer books make it clear that partaking of Holy Communion is compulsory. The first prayer book states that this is a duty to be performed at least once a year (1549, para. 17) and the second changes this to three times a year, including Easter (1552, para. 22). The first prayer book (but not the second) states that parishioners who, for no adequate reason, 'doth absent themselves, or doth ungodly in the Parish church occupy themselves' shall be excommunicate (barred from communion, trade and fellowship with other Christians) by the ecclesiastical courts (1549, para.17; 1552, para. 22). This was probably because the second Edwardian Act of Uniformity provided for secular punishment of lay people who did not comply, whereas the first Act of Uniformity omitted to do so.

It should be clear that the statements in the prayer book of 1549 were ambiguous in their approach: the sacraments of the bread and wine were the body and blood of Christ in some way, but the precise nature of that sense is left unclear. The first prayer book's authors believed not in transubstantiation (where the bread and wine transformed on consecration into the body and blood of Jesus) as did Catholics, nor yet in the real presence of Christ in the Sacraments as did Luther, but apparently followed the views of the ninth-century Benedictine monk Ratramnus of Corbie, whose *Of the Body and Blood of Christ* had been reprinted in Cologne in 1531 and in Geneva in 1541. Nicholas Ridley, who had great influence on Cranmer, certainly believed with Ratramnus that the communion involved dual and simultaneous operations – the body received bread and wine; the spirit received the body and blood of Christ present spiritually. Cranmer left the wording so ambiguous that even Bishop Gardiner, a conservative Catholic, felt that he could without qualms use Cranmer's words of consecration and administration. The second prayer book came down more boldly on the side of the Zwinglian view that the bread and wine had a memorial meaning only. The priest of the 1549 book offers a sacrifice; the minister of the 1552 book administers the bread and wine as a memorial act. In 1549, the priest stands 'afore the altar' (a word associated with sacrifice). The celebrant in 1552 is ordered to stand behind the 'table' facing the people. The Black Rubric of the 1552 book elaborated on this – the bread and wine remind the communicant of the blessings accorded them by Christ's death on the cross but they in no way signify worship of the bread and wine or any belief in 'any real and essential presence there being of Christ's natural flesh and blood.' It is superstitious to believe anything else (1552, para. 23). (See the *Visual Sources Book*, Plate 7.5a and b, for examples of the chalice for the Mass and the cup for communion.)

Summary

What have we just discovered from a close reading of these two documents?

1   The state was ordering what Christians should believe and how they should worship. At this time, the nature of the church's teaching or doctrine could and did change rapidly. Attending communion was compulsory. You could not exercise consumer choice. You had to attend your parish church. Not to do so meant that you would be thrust out of the community.

2   Only a close reading of both documents reveals the radical change in official belief reflected within them.

3   These documents represent a struggle at the centre about the nature of the doctrinal changes brought about by reformation. They show that, by the end of Edward's reign, the radical Protestants had triumphed. These changes reflect the transformation of the early English Reformation from a Lutheran movement into a church with doctrines close to those of Zwingli. Historians need to develop a good knowledge of contemporary doctrinal positions in order to make sense of this debate.

4   The documents are prescriptive rather than descriptive in nature. They order what people should believe and how this service should be held and regarded. Historians need to look elsewhere to discover whether these instructions were followed and whether people really did believe the church's official teaching.

5   Cumulatively, both documents emphasise that Protestantism is a religion of the Word. The drama of the old liturgy is being replaced bit by bit, by thorough Bible reading, by a plainer service of Holy Communion that excludes any suggestion of sacrifice and adoration. (Edward's commissioners toured the country's churches to ensure that chantry chapels with their side altars, and all rood lofts, roods, holy sepulchres, figures of saints and stained glass windows were obliterated. See the *Visual Sources Book*, Plate 7.10, which shows how Biblical texts replaced images in Edwardian and Elizabethan churches).

Reigns of Mary and Elizabeth I

As Wallace says, Edward's older sister Mary restored the spiritual authority of the papacy as soon as she was able. She also undid the legislation of Edward regarding uniformity under the prayer book and brought back the heresy laws. Traditionalist bishops such as Gardiner and Bonner were restored to freedom and favour. Her reign is noted for the martyrdom of some leading ecclesiastics (notably Cranmer, Ridley and Latimer) and many ordinary Protestants. In addition, many Protestants fled the kingdom into exile in Germany and Switzerland. A few pockets of Protestantism survived in the shape of secret congregations, such as those in London and Ipswich.

Thomas Cranmer (1489–1556) (see Figure 8.7) was educated at the University of Cambridge. In 1529 he wrote a treatise defending Henry VIII's divorce from Catharine of Aragon, and in 1530 he was part of the embassy to Charles V. When he returned to England in 1533, it was as archbishop of Canterbury. He thereupon pronounced the royal divorce, declared Henry's marriage to Anne Boleyn lawful and defended the royal supremacy over the Church of England. He was very much Henry's man from then on, declaring null and void Henry's marriage to Anne in 1536, supporting the divorce from Anne of Cleves in 1539 and not rushing to Cromwell's aid in 1540. However, he did unsuccessfully oppose the harsh Six Articles in 1539, and in 1542 he defended the Great Bible against Bishop Gardiner and was cleared of charges of heresy by Henry himself. Under Edward VI, he was a member of Edward's privy council. He chaired production of the first Edwardian prayer book in 1548 (which was based on a vernacular version of the Catholic services) and was instrumental in radical revisions of the prayer book in 1552. He was to the fore in proposing a thorough-going reform of church law (*Reformatio legum ecclesiasticarum*) and promulgating the 1552 forty-two articles of religion. He signed Edward VI's will that barred his sister Mary from the succession and in 1553 supported Queen Jane Grey against Mary. It was unsurprising that Mary and Cardinal Pole regarded him as their arch enemy and, when Cranmer refused to recognise papal jurisdiction, he was condemned as a heretic. In 1556, under torture, Cranmer recanted all but his rejection of the doctrine of transubstantiation. When he was burnt at the stake in Oxford on 21 March 1556, he regretted and repudiated his recantation.

It is important to note that, although Mary restored the papal authority, she was unable to reverse key aspects of the crown's reformation of the church – for example, the dissolution of the monasteries and chantries achieved under Henry and Edward. This was because the lands and property of the monasteries had been distributed to the crown and to the landed classes, who had a vested interest in the policy as a result.

While by no means all Protestants were martyred or actively persecuted under Mary, it is possible to see in her policy the seeds of the eventual Protestantisation of England. Under Elizabeth, John Foxe's *Acts and Monuments* memorialised and publicised the deeds of the queen and the English martyrs in such a way that neither would be forgotten. The experience of exile enjoyed by over 800 people had a profound effect on the nature of Elizabethan Protestantism, bringing so many of its ecclesiastics under continental influence. The Zwinglian, and especially the Calvinist, elements that were gathering strength in the closing phase of the previous reign were accentuated during an exile spent with churches that had rejected episcopacy and evolved systems of church government that abandoned priesthood and

Figure 8.7   Gerlach Flicke, *Thomas Cranmer*, 1545, oil on panel, 98.4 x 76.2 cm.
Photo: © National Portrait Gallery, London

vestments (ceremonial clothing) and ceremonies regarded as 'popish', or worse, and accorded the laity a greater part in worship and congregational government. Some of the most important controversies that characterised the Elizabethan church were foreshadowed during the exile: for instance, the Knoxians at Frankfurt (led by the Scottish reformer John Knox) and the Coxians (led by Richard Cox) had an acrimonious debate in 1555 regarding the use of ecclesiastical vestments in the reformed church. As a result of Cox's victory, Knox left Frankfurt for Geneva.

The Elizabethan settlement

You should already have read and made notes on pp. 133–7 of your set book. This reading will help you to make sense of what follows.

When Mary died in 1558, she was succeeded by her half-sister Elizabeth. The Marian exiles and the covert Protestant congregations within England had great expectations of Elizabeth's reign. She became the heroine of Foxe's *Book of Martyrs*. (Anthology Document 2.19, 'Come over the Born, Bessy', is one of the ballads circulated in her honour.) It is true that Elizabeth, as daughter of Henry and Anne Boleyn, had a vested interest in preserving the Henrician Reformation and denying the pope's jurisdiction. At the beginning, parliament repealed the religious legislation of Mary's reign, approved an Act of Supremacy and named Elizabeth as supreme governor of the church (see the *Visual Sources Book*, Plate 7.6). An Act of Uniformity compelling the use of the liturgies of Edward VI, including the radical 1552 prayer book, seemed to consolidate the Edwardian Reformation. There seems no doubt, however, that her own preference was for an episcopal church that followed many of the practices of the Henrician Church of England. She also had a personal antipathy towards some of the reformers – especially John Knox (who had recently trumpeted his dislike of women governors) and John Calvin. Protestants were shocked when the host was raised for adoration at Mass in the Chapel Royal and the crucifix continued to be used. In 1559, the wording of the Book of Common Prayer was modified to make the beliefs about Holy Communion (Eucharist) much vaguer and, therefore, easier for believers of many different persuasions to accept. The communion rail separated the chancel from the nave, and ecclesiastical vestments and images of saints were retained.

Elizabeth's religious policy during the first part of her reign seems to have been designed to try to accommodate Catholics and Protestants of many shades of opinion. For example, the Act of Supremacy used more moderate language than the Henrician and Edwardian legislation and declared that the monarch was supreme governor of the church and not supreme head (Anthology Document 2.14, 'Acts of Supremacy, 1534 and 1559'). Whatever her personal beliefs, Elizabeth's principal concern was to secure her throne and the undivided loyalty of her subjects. (Plate 7.7 in the *Visual Sources Book* is a contemporary genealogy showing Elizabeth's descent from King Rollo – another example of her concern to establish her title to the throne.) Sovereignty was all-important. It was unnecessary to have a window into men's souls. Unfortunately, many of her subjects were not content with this: they wanted patio doors. In 1570, the pope made it difficult for Catholics to comply with the royal command that all her subjects should swear an oath of fealty and uniformity by declaring that the queen was illegitimate and excommunicated, and by releasing all Catholics from any obligation of loyalty towards her. Thereafter the church authorities found it difficult to compel

Catholics to attend their parish churches and receive communion. Until the 1580s, such recusants were not actively persecuted. The uncovering of some Catholic plots against the crown and the threat of invasion by a Catholic power led to more vigorous persecution.

On the other hand, the radical Protestants wanted to reform the church even further. Many of these radicals were the very ecclesiastics that Elizabeth had to appoint to senior positions in the church in the 1560s. To her dismay, not one of the surviving Marian bishops would agree to serve under Elizabeth.

The vestiarian controversy

Protestants had agreed to serve the queen because they did not wish control of the church to pass to conservative elements. They hoped to mould the settlement from within and to make the Church of England a reformed church on the continental model of which they had first-hand knowledge. Former exiles (such as John Jewel) had high hopes when, in the summer and autumn of 1559, they served as royal commissioners and toured England, administered the oath of supremacy and purified the church of what they saw as idolatrous and superstitious monuments and practices. They felt let down by the queen's adherence to ceremonies and some of the more radical among them agonised over the importance or otherwise of images and crucifixes. Thomas Sampson and John Jewel both concluded that, rather than agree to use these images, they should reject or relinquish appointments as bishops.

It was a clause in the 1559 Act of Uniformity that retained clerical vestments as they had been at the start of Edward's reign that sparked off a major dispute between the queen and her churchmen. Edwin Sandys, bishop of Worcester, felt sure that the use of these vestments would not be enforced. 'Only the popish vestments remain in our church, I mean the copes; which, however, we hope will not last very long.'[3] His belief seemed to be borne out by the remarkable latitude permitted the clergy at the start of the reign.

The importance of clerical dress

As you saw in Block 1, medieval people thought that each person's dress should reflect his or her class and occupation, and there were laws to enforce this. This idea was also prevalent in the early modern period. Protestants (particularly those of the Calvinist and Zwinglian persuasions) were considerably exercised by the issue of clerical dress. They believed that the ornate vestments worn by Catholic clergy denoted a sacrificial priesthood. See the *Visual Sources Book*, Plates 7.8 and 7.9, and Figures 8.8 and 8.9 for the Catholic clerical dress to which Protestants objected. See Figures 8.10 and 8.11 for the plain dress favoured by both continental and English Protestants.

---

[3] Edwin Sandys to Peter Martyr, 1 April 1560 (Robinson, 1842, pp. 72–5).

Unfortunately, no contemporary woodcuts survive showing the precise clerical uniform prescribed by Archbishop Parker in the 1560s. We are forced to rely on rather unsatisfactory verbal descriptions and portraits such as those of Matthew Parker (Figure 8.4), Edmund Grindal (Figure 8.10) and Heinrich Bullinger (Figure 8.11).

Then, in January 1565, Elizabeth rebuked her first archbishop of Canterbury, Matthew Parker, for the lack of conformity in outward matters in the church, enjoining the vestments clause. Parker was left to bring his clergy into conformity. The clergy were ordered to wear the round cap and surplice. Resistance was strong at the universities of Oxford and Cambridge and in London. At Oxford, Thomas Sampson and Lawrence Humphrey led the field. It was feared, in 1565, that up to forty London parish clergy would refuse to officiate at the most important feast of the Christian year – Easter – rather than

Figure 8.8 Clerical dress, alb and stole, secured by the girdle, amice still over the head, from P.S. Barnwell, Claire Cross and Ann Rycraft (2005) *Mass and Parish in Late Medieval England: The Use of York*, Reading: Spire Books. Photo: © Allan B. Barton

Figure 8.9 Clerical dress, chasuble, showing Y-shaped orphreys on front, from P.S. Barnwell, Claire Cross and Ann Rycraft (2005) *Mass and Parish in Late Medieval England: The Use of York*, Reading: Spire Books. Photo: © Allan B. Barton

Figure 8.10 Unknown artist, *Edmund Grindal, Archbishop of Canterbury*, aged 61, 1580, Elizabethan Protestants, especially those who had been in continental exile under Mary, favoured the simple attire of cap and gown for ministers (including bishops and archbishops). Photo: © Lambeth Palace Library, London

wear the costume. In the event, some clergy (including Sampson) were deprived (removed from their church livings) and some London citizens' wives took to the streets in support of the rebels.

Yet the resistance was not as strong as Archbishop Parker had feared. Many churchmen agreed with Sandys and Jewel that resistance in this matter involved resistance to the royal authority. Both men saw the vestments issue as a minor matter. The true gospel was still preached 'freely and faithfully'.

HENRICVS   BVLLINGERVS.

SIc candor, pietas, sic & doctrina relucent,
  Bullingere, tuo semper in ore simul.
Quam doctus fueris, pius, & candoris amicus,
  Sat tua scripta probant, candida, docta, pia.

Figure 8.11   Unknown artist, *Heinrich (Henry) Bullinger*, engraving on paper, 17.7 x 12.6 cm. Germanisches Nationalmuseum, Nuremberg, Graphische Sammlung Mp 3216. Bullinger was revered by the Marian exiles. When they returned to England after Elizabeth's accession, they continued to correspond with Bullinger and value his judgements on the Elizabethan settlement of religion. Photo: © Germanisches Nationalmuseum

Sampson and Humphrey were blowing up the issue out of all proportion. They preferred to leave the gospel unpreached rather than to wear the vestments. Sandys and Jewel saw this as inappropriate. Compared with the need for the gospel, this was a 'thing indifferent' and certainly not a resigning matter.

Summary

It is clear that both Sampson and Humphrey were concerned about the wider implications of the controversy. If the royal supremacy meant that churchmen had to agree, against their consciences, to reintroduce unscriptural ceremonies and practices into the church, this was to their minds intolerable. Yet worse was the fact that the monarch was seeking to alter the church without the agreement of churchmen.

The vestiarian controversy demonstrates clearly the practical conflict that existed between the queen's conception of the church (and of her role as its supreme governor) and that of many of its personnel. These individuals handled the conflict in various ways: some bowed to the queen's will in the interest of retaining influence within the church; others effectively bowed out. In either case, the queen had her way and enforced her will.

This controversy shows how closely our two themes of the formation of the state and of religious beliefs and ideologies were intertwined.

You might understandably now have the impression that Elizabeth was able to impose her religious settlement on the Church of England successfully and that she did this without the consent of most churchmen. In fact, however, Elizabeth was far from controlling her church in such a crude manner. She did succeed in retaining the cap, gown and surplice as the required clerical costume, but she never pushed the issue of the use of the full Eucharistic vestments. She relied on her bishops, archdeacons and deans to enforce compliance, and we know that enforcement was never 100 per cent successful (see the *Visual Sources Book*, Plates 7.3, 7.5).

There were other ways of 'reforming' the church than by rewriting the canons (laws) of the church or by parliamentary legislation. Take the case of the suppression of the prophesying. Elizabeth thought that these preaching conferences were subversive and ordered her next archbishop of Canterbury, Edmund Grindal (see Figure 8.10), to suppress them. When he refused, she suspended him from his duties. On the surface, it looked as though the queen's policies had won through. Prophesyings were forbidden. Grindal's replacement, John Whitgift, was appointed in 1583 to put the church in order and rout the zealous hot Protestant (puritan) element. In 1583–84, the ministers were required to take an oath of conformity. In 1589–90, there was a determined assault on ministerial conferences within the church. But what *effect* did all this have? Prophesyings were never suppressed in the northern province (Yorkshire, Lancashire, Cumberland, Durham, Northumberland), and in the south they resurfaced as 'lectures by combination'. Throughout the country there were diocesan regimes that saw the preaching ministry as an important agent in the Protestantisation of the people and were unwilling to take a Whitgiftian hard line against such men. Moreover, strong support for Protestantism among the ruling classes forced Whitgift to moderate his own stance. The form of subscription finally adopted permitted most ministers to keep their livings. Ringleaders were removed but most puritan ministers were left unscathed in 1589–90.

The success of more advanced Protestantism – of Grindalian churchmanship, as some describe it – depended on the conversion of large sections of the population, especially of the ruling groups. Success depended on success! The more that the people wanted a church that looked like a Protestant rather than a Catholic church, the more difficult it became for the queen and her ministers to give them anything less. (See Plate 7.10 in the *Visual Sources Book*. The replacement of images in the church by the visual severity of texts from Scripture reinforces the sea-change in worship and its setting. Note, however, that the arrangement of the texts echoed that of the painted triptychs that adorned medieval altars and that the effect was still decorative.) The queen and Whitgift may have believed that they could impose a settlement, but on the ground the settlement was a matter of negotiation between the church and the laity – between bishops and clergy, between clergy and laity, between bishops and local notability.

CONCLUSION

The issues that have been discussed in this unit all touch on the themes of state formation and belief and ideologies. We have seen how Henry VIII and two of his children asserted their sovereign control over all their subjects, whether lay or ecclesiastical. (Even Mary, in reinstating the papal supremacy, unintentionally demonstrated that secular legislation could achieve such a profound effect.) We have discussed why they did this and have learned something of the nature of the English state in so doing. We have considered religious change. We have considered whether the crown's authority over its subjects was as absolute in spiritual matters as it wished. But don't forget that we have also considered aspects of the historian's craft along the way, discussing how debates among historians may deepen our understanding of historical processes.

REFERENCES

Bowker, M. (1981) *The Henrician Reformation in the Diocese of Lincoln under John Longland, 1521–1547*, Cambridge, Cambridge University Press.

Brigden, S. (1989) *London and the Reformation,* Oxford, Oxford University Press.

Clark, P. (1977) *English Provincial Society from the Reformation to the Revolution. Religion, Politics and Society in Kent, 1500–1640*, Hassocks, Harvester Press.

Cross, M.C (1976) *Church and People 1450–1660. The Triumph of the Laity in the English Church,* London, Fontana.

Cross, M.C. (1982) 'The development of Protestantism in Leeds and Hull, 1520–1640: the evidence from wills', *Northern History*, vol. 18, pp. 230–8.

Davies, C.S.L. (1976) *Peace, Print and Protestantism, 1450–1558*, London, Paladin.

Davis, J.F. (1983) *Heresy and Reformation in the South-East of England, 1520–1559*, London, Royal Historical Society.

Dickens, A.G. (1959a) *Lollards and Protestants in the Diocese of York, 1509–1558*, Oxford, Oxford University Press.

Dickens, A.G. (1959b) *Thomas Cromwell and the English Reformation*, London, English Universities Press.

Dickens, A.G. (1989) *The English Reformation*, revised edn, London, Batsford.

Duffy, E. (1992) *The Stripping of the Altars: Traditional Religion in England, 1400–1580*, New Haven/London, Yale University Press.

Duffy, E. (2001) *The Voices of Morebath: Reformation and Rebellion in an English Village*, New Haven/London, Yale University Press.

Elton, G.R. (1955) *England under the Tudors*, London, Methuen.

Elton, G.R. (1960) *The Tudor Constitution*, Cambridge, Cambridge University Press.

Elton, G.R. (1962) *Henry VIII: An Essay in Revision*, London, Historical Association.

Elton, G.R. (1972) *Policy and Police: Enforcement of the Reformation in the Age of Thomas Cromwell*, Cambridge, Cambridge University Press.

Haigh, C. (1975) *Reformation and Resistance in Tudor Lancashire*, Cambridge, Cambridge University Press.

Haigh, C. (1983) 'Anticlericalism and the English Reformation', *History*, vol. 68, pp. 391–407.

Haigh, C. (1993) *English Reformations*, Oxford, Oxford University Press.

Hurstfield, J. (1973) *Freedom, Corruption and Government in Elizabethan England*, London, Jonathan Cape.

Jordan, W.K. (1961) *The Charities of Rural England 1480–1660. The Aspirations and the Achievements of the Rural Society*, New York, Russell Sage Foundation.

Lander, S. (1976) 'Church courts and the Reformation in the diocese of Chichester, 1500–1558' in O'Day, R. and Heal, F. (eds) *Continuity and Change: Personnel and Administration of the Church in England, 1500–1642*, Leicester, Leicester University Press, pp. 215–37.

Mahew, G.J. (1983) 'The progress of the Reformation in East Sussex, 1530–1559: the evidence from wills', *Southern History*, vol. 5, pp. 38–67.

Robinson, H. (1842) (ed.) *The Zurich Letters, Comprising the Correspondence of Several English Bishops and Others, With Some of the Helvetian Reformers, During the Early Part of the Reign of Queen Elizabeth*, vol. 1, Cambridge, Parker Society.

Scarisbrick, J.J. (1968) *Henry VIII*, London, Eyre & Spottiswoode.

Scarisbrick, J.J. (1984) *The Reformation and the English People*, Oxford, Blackwell.

Sheils, W.J. (1976) 'Some problems of government in a new diocese: the Bishop and the Puritans in the Diocese of Peterborough, 1560–1630' in O'Day, R. and Heal, F. (eds) *Continuity and Change*, Leicester, Leicester University Press, pp. 167–87.

Sheils, W.J. (1979) 'The Puritans in the Diocese of Peterborough, 1558–1610', *Northampton Record Society*, vol. 30, pp. 51–66.

Spufford, M. (1971) 'The scribes of villagers' wills in the sixteenth and seventeenth centuries and their influence', *Local Population Studies*, vol. 7, pp. 29–43.

Spufford, M. (1974) *Contrasting Communities*, Cambridge, Cambridge University Press.

Trevelyan, G.M. (1926) *History of England*, London, Longman.

Williams, P. (1979) *The Tudor Regime*, Oxford, Oxford University Press.

Donna Loftus

To end this unit, I would like you to reflect on a debate that was touched on at the end of Unit 6, 'Women and the Reformation'. As you may remember from reading this section, while some historians, such as Steven Ozment (1993), argue that the Reformation provided new opportunities for women by enhancing the value of marriage, others, such as Lyndal Roper (1989), argue that the closure of nunneries limited opportunities for women's piety and independence. For the purposes of consolidating your work on this block, exploring this debate can be helpful in illustrating the complex social and political impact of the Reformation.

EXERCISE

Read Anthology Document 2.12, 'Marie Dentière's letter to Queen Marguerite of Navarre, 1539', and answer the following question:

According to Dentière, does the evangelical rediscovery of the Gospel have any significance for women?

Spend about 15 minutes on this exercise.

SPECIMEN ANSWER

Yes, it liberated women as well as men.

DISCUSSION

According to Dentière, men and women are obliged to spread the evangelical message. She emphasises that there are not two Gospels – one for men and one for women – but only one. Women may not be permitted to preach, but if they have been given the grace by God, they should spread the Gospel among themselves through the spoken, as well as the written, word. As a result, she hopes that women in future 'will not be so much despised as in the past'.

Dentière used Reformation ideas to defend women's ability to read and interpret the Scriptures. However, her pamphlets were confiscated by the reformers she supported in Geneva. The Reformation challenged fundamental ideas about the social order and people's roles and, as the treatment of Dentière shows, new ideas about appropriate behaviour soon emerged. Historians continue to debate the extent to which the Reformation shaped gender relations, and questions about who is qualified to interpret and preach the word of God are still matters of concern.

After studying this block you are now aware that the Reformation is more than a religious squabble that was important over 500 years ago but has little relevance today. The Reformation in Europe certainly resulted in a major religious split between a Catholic south and a Protestant north, but it also served to transform the social, cultural and political landscape of Europe. It led to a century of political unrest, civil wars and warfare across most of north-western Europe, not to mention major population movements towards the end of the sixteenth century. It is, in other words, much more than a purely religious split. You will also have realised that the Reformation is often impossible to separate from the major political, social and economic issues of the day. Early modern beliefs and ideologies clearly had important consequences for European state formation, and in some cases affected the relationship between producers and consumers. The Dutch revolt, for instance, was never solely about religion, as initially expressed in the quest for toleration of the reformed faith in particular, but just as much about political freedom and objections to economic exploitation. It was a rebellion against religious repression and taxation, as well as the creation of a centralised state governed through Brussels and controlled from Spain by its Habsburg rulers.

The Reformation was a challenge to the hegemony of the Catholic Church but the reformers had to establish their own legitimacy. Urban centres were crucial in this regard; the expansion of printing and growing networks of scholars allowed ideas to circulate. As you saw in the case of Geneva, municipal authorities could also provide the structures necessary to enforce new ideas and practices associated with reformation. It is difficult to know how people felt about reform and whether their support for it was part of a broader expression of dissatisfaction with political and religious orthodoxy, or if opposition was an expression of political allegiances as much as religious beliefs. As you saw in relation to the Peasants' War and the Reformation in England, historians continue to debate the relationship between clamours for religious reform and desires for social and political change. As all of these cases show, in the history of the Reformation worldly and spiritual issues are closely combined, and differences of historical interpretation can result from differences in emphasis. You may have noticed this when comparing the block with the set book by Wallace. Whereas Unit 7, for example, underlines the role of reformed faith in driving and sustaining the Dutch revolt, Wallace puts greater emphasis on its political aspects.

As you saw in the historiographical debates on the Reformation in England that you covered in Unit 8, perspectives can vary according to the focus of historians, the questions they pose and the sources they use. Elton and Hurstfield explored the Reformation through political and administrative systems and used sources such as parliamentary bills. However, the debates that ensued about the causes of the Reformation in England helped to inspire new approaches and generate new questions. The local studies that you were introduced to in Unit 8 were undertaken by historians who responded to these questions by devising methods and approaches that enabled them to test the extent of genuine popularity of the Reformation in England. For example, as you saw, many local studies used wills to determine the religious beliefs of the population. Since then there have been a number of studies debating the continuing strength of Catholicism in the sixteenth century (Duffy, 1992). Historical knowledge develops through debates and, although historians may strongly disagree at times, they are involved in a collaborative discipline involving studies that continue to build on one another.

The challenge to authority inherent in the Reformation, with its rejection of the authority of the Catholic Church and the pope, and its emphasis on the Bible as the sole authority, available to all in the vernacular, is seen by some scholars as laying the foundation for many of the political structures and social values we are familiar with today. As you discovered in Unit 5, Weber posed questions about the extent that Protestantism facilitated the developments towards capitalism and modernity. And as you saw in Unit 8, historians such as Elton, writing in the 1960s, argued that the Reformation in England instigated the political developments that eventually led to political reform. As you move on through the module, you may want to think about other events and processes that have been influenced by the Reformation. In Block 3 you will study the relationship between political and religious affiliations in the Civil Wars of the seventeenth century, and in Block 4 you will see how religious ideas influenced attitudes to slavery. However, in the study of history, there is a need to balance perspectives that focus on explaining change over time with those that seek to understand events such as the Reformation on its own terms and in its own history.

REFERENCES

Duffy, E. (1992) *The Stripping of the Altars: Traditional Religion in England 1400–1580*, New Haven/London, Yale University Press.

Ozment, S. (1993) *Protestants. The Birth of a Revolution*, London, Fontana.

Roper, L. (1989) *The Holy Household: Women and Morals in Reformation Augsburg*, Oxford, Clarendon Press.

FURTHER READING

Unit 6

Abray, L.J. (1985) *The People's Reformation. Magistrates, Clergy and Commons in Strasbourg, 1500–1598*, Oxford, Basil Blackwell.

Collinson, P. (2003) *The Reformation*, London, Weidenfeld & Nicolson.

Pettegree, A. (2005) *The Culture of Persuasion in the European Reformation*, Cambridge University Press, Cambridge.

Russell, P.A. (1986) *Lay Theology in the Reformation. Popular Pamphleteers in Southwest Germany 1521–1525*, Cambridge, Cambridge University Press.

Unit 7

Duke, A. (1990) *Reformation and Revolt in the Low Countries*, London, Hambledon Press.

Duke, A., Lewis, G. and Pettegree, A. (eds.) (1992) *Calvinism in Europe 1540–1610*, Manchester, Manchester University Press.

DuPlessis, R.S. (1991) *Lille and the Dutch Revolt*, Cambridge, Cambridge University Press.

Grell, O.P. (1989) *Dutch Calvinists in Early Stuart London. The Dutch Church in Austin Friars, 1603–1642*, Leiden, Brill.

Israel, J.I. (1995) *The Dutch Republic. Its Rise, Greatness, and Fall 1477–1806*, Oxford, Oxford University Press.

Kossmann, E.H. and Mellink, A.F. (eds) (1974) *Texts Concerning the Revolt of the Netherlands*, Cambridge, Cambridge University Press.

Lewis, G. (1985) 'Calvinism in Geneva in the Time of Calvin and Beza, 1541–1608', in Prestwich, M. (ed.) *International Calvinism 1541–1715*, Oxford, Oxford University Press.

Marnef, G. (1996) *Antwerp in the Age of Reformation. Underground Protestantism in a Commercial Metropolis*, Baltimore, Johns Hopkins University Press.

Naphy, W.G. (1994) *Calvin and the Consolidation of the Genevan Reformation*, Manchester, Manchester University Press.

Pettegree, A. (1992) *Emden and the Dutch Revolt. Exile and the Development of Reformed Protestantism*, Oxford, Clarendon Press.

Rott, J. (1994) 'The Strasbourg Kirchenpfleger and parish discipline: theory and practice' in Wright, D.F. (ed.) *Martin Bucer. Reforming Church and Community*, Cambridge, Cambridge University Press.

Spierling, K.E. (2005) *Infant Baptism in Reformation Geneva. The Shaping of a Community, 1536–1564*, Aldershot, Ashgate.

Tanis, J. and Horst, D. (1993) *Images of Discord. A Graphic Interpretation of the Opening Decades of the Eighty Years' War*, Grand Rapids, W.B. Eerdmans.

Unit 8

If you are interested and have time, you may dip into any of the following works with profit.

Barnwell, P.S., Cross, C. and Rycraft, A. (2005) *Mass and Parish in Late Medieval England: The Use of York*, Reading, Spire Books.

Bernard, G.W. (1993) 'Anne Boleyn's Religion', *Historical Journal*, vol. 36, pp. 1–20.

Bernard, G.W. (1998) 'Elton's Cromwell', *History,* vol. 83, pp. 587–607.

Bernard, G.W. (2005) *The King's Reformation: Henry VIII and the Remaking of the English Church,* New Haven/London, Yale University Press.

Bernard, G.W. (2007) *The King's Reformation*, New Haven, Yale University Press.

Collinson, P. (1982) *The Religion of Protestants,* Oxford, Oxford University Press.

Collinson, P. (1988) *The Birthpangs of Protestant England*, Oxford, Oxford University Press.

Collinson, P. (2003) *The Reformation*, London, Weidenfeld & Nicolson.

Dickens, A.G. (1959) *Thomas Cromwell and the English Reformation*, London, English Universities Press.

Dickens, A.G. (1989) *The English Reformation*, London, Batsford.

Duffy, E. (1992) *The Stripping of the Altars: Traditional Religion in England, 1400–1580*, New Haven/London, Yale University Press.

Elton, G.R. (1960) *The Tudor Constitution*, Cambridge, Cambridge University Press.

Elton, G.R. (1973) *Reform and Renewal: Thomas Cromwell and the Common Weal*, Cambridge, Cambridge University Press.

Elton, G.R. (1974–92) *Studies in Tudor and Stuart Politics and Government*, 4 vols, Cambridge, Cambridge University Press.

Haigh, C. (1993) *English Reformations: Religion and Society under the Tudors*, Oxford, Oxford University Press.

Heal, F. and O'Day, R. (eds) (1977) *Church and Society in England. Henry VIII to James I*, London, Macmillan.

O'Day, R. (1972) 'Thomas Bentham: a case study in the problems of the early Elizabethan episcopate', *Journal of Ecclesiastical History,* vol. 23, pp. 137–59.

O'Day, R. (1986) *The Debate on the English Reformation*, London, Methuen.

MacCulloch, D. (1996) *Thomas Cranmer*, New Haven/London, Yale University Press.

Scarisbrick, J.J. (1984) *The Reformation and the English People*, Oxford, Blackwell.

Spufford, M. (1971) 'The scribes of villagers' wills in the sixteenth and seventeenth centuries and their influence', *Local Population Studies*, vol. 7, pp. 29–43.

Zell, M.L. (1977) 'The use of religious preambles', *Bulletin of the Institute of Historical Research*, vol. 50, pp. 246–9.

GLOSSARY

(N.B. Some relevant items will be found in the glossary for Block 1)

Act of Parliament (Statute): legislation that received the assent of both Houses of Parliament and the monarch before being placed on the statute book.

Anabaptist: member of a Protestant sect that rejected infant baptism, sought rebaptism of adults and establishment of Christian communism.

apocalyptic: a belief held by some reformers that these were the last days before Christ's second coming, heralded by famine, war and disease as foretold in the Book of Revelation in the Bible. The pope was identified with Ant_christ.

beeldenstorm: **iconoclasm** in the Netherlands.

bill: the proposal stage of an **Act of Parliament**.

broadside: a paper printed on one side with news, notices and songs. Broadsides were a popular form for the circulation of news. They could be read aloud or pinned on walls and they often contained images from woodcuts.

burghers: citizens of towns and cities. In the early modern period these were usually the local middle classes.

Calvinism: Protestant denomination or **confession** primarily associated with the reformer John Calvin, which emphasises **predestination** and the sovereignty of God.

Calvinist: see **Calvinism**.

chalice: cup used for the wine at communion.

chancery: an administrative body and court with the power to make law.

chantry chapels: parts of a church or cathedral set aside for the chanting (singing) of **masses** for the dead. Also known as chantries.

chiliastic: from chiliasm, the doctrine that Christ on his return will reign upon earth for a thousand years before the end of the world.

confession/confessional: the set of beliefs that unites one group of believers and separates them from other groups.

convocation: the ancient assemblies of the clergy of the Church of England divided into the provincial convocations of Canterbury and York.

deprived: loss of position within the church.

'Donation of Constantine': it claimed to be a fourth-century grant from Emperor Constantine I, a convert to Christianity, awarding the pope control over the Christian world. It was judged by **humanists** to be a forgery from the eighth century.

ecclesiastical: adjective derived from the word for church.

edict: authoritative order/declaration.

elector: prince, lay or clerical, within the Holy Roman Empire who has the right to participate in the election of the emperor.

episcopacy: system of church government by bishops.

episcopal: of or pertaining to bishops.

episcopalian church: a church with bishops. The Scottish Episcopalian Church was part of the wider Anglican community outside Scotland.

eschatology: branch of **theology** addressing the end of the world.

evangelical: Christianity based on the gospels or membership of a Protestant sect emphasising personal conversion and belief in justification (salvation) by faith in Christ's redeeming death on the cross.

hegemony: the dominance of one group over another. The term refers to the way that groups use culture to promote their understanding of the world as natural and normal.

Huguenots: French **Calvinists**.

humanism: Renaissance cultural movement based on study of the classics. Christian humanists applied these principles of study to the Bible.

humanist: see **humanism**.

iconoclasm: destruction of images.

magistracy: secular rulers.

Mass: from the words of dismissal at the end of the Latin service: *missa est*. Celebration of the Eucharist or Holy Communion in a Roman Catholic Church. There were different versions: high (full ceremonial); low; dry (no celebration of the communion).

oligarchy: government by a small group of individuals; an oligarch is the ruler or figurehead of an oligarchy.

Parousia: the second coming of Christ.

parson: an Anglican cleric with full responsibility for a parish.

philology: from the Greek for 'love of language' – to be understood as **humanist** engagement in linguistics and biblical criticism, or exegesis.

predestination: the belief, often but not exclusively associated with Calvin, that God has determined who will be saved irrespective of personal merits.

prophesying: revealing the word of God to the public.

Roman Inquisition: established in 1542 to combat Protestantism and act against heresy, especially in Italy – part of the Counter-Reformation measures taken by the papacy.

satire: a classical form of expression that used ridicule to critique beliefs and practices. The **humanist** revival of interest in Ancient Greek texts led to the rebirth of satire.

spiritualty: religious arm of the state.

temporalty: secular arm of the state.

theology: the study of religion and religious doctrine.

tithe: a tax paid to the church.

vernacular tongue: native, popular language.

vicar substitute: commonly used to describe the clergyman who was appointed by an **ecclesiastical** patron (monastery, bishop, cathedral) to serve a parish. To be contrasted with a rector, who had a right to the valuable great **tithes** of the parish.

vicar-general: the monarch's substitute (or delegate) in ruling the church.

Walloon: French dialect spoken in parts of Belgium.

Walloons: French people living in south Belgium and adjacent parts of France.

INDEX